"*What Is a Healthy Church Member?* fills an enormous gap in the literature of practical Christian living. The book is extremely valuable as a straightforward, easy-to-read user's guide to the church. It is also a profound and thoroughly biblical digest of practical ecclesiology, written with a compelling sense of passion and urgency. As such, it is a valuable resource for every church member—from the beginner to the seasoned pastor alike. In an era when Christians in general seem confused about what kind of community the church ought to be, here's a helpful handbook outlining the church's true biblical priorities, especially as they apply to individual church members."
> —JOHN MACARTHUR, President, Grace to You

"Thabiti Anyabwile has filled a great void in contemporary Christian literature. Books on how to be a faithful pastor or church leader are common, but it is rare to find a book that speaks so directly about being a faithful church member. With a wealth of biblical insight and practical instruction, Anyabwile calls Christians to do more than just attend church, but to be the kind of faithful, engaged church members that God intends them to be. Given the state of so many of our churches today, this book arrives not a moment too soon."
> —R. ALBERT MOHLER JR., President,
> The Southern Baptist Theological Seminary

"Some books are so simple they are scarcely worth skimming; others are so complex that, unless their subject matter is extraordinarily important, they are not worth the time they demand. But sometimes one finds a book that is simultaneously simple and profound—and this is one of them. In a generation when many people are talking about the importance of Christians living "in community," few have unpacked, in biblically faithful and personally penetrating ways, just what that means. Thabiti Anyabwile closes the gap. Read it, think about it, pray over it—and distribute it generously around your congregation."
> —D. A. CARSON, Research Professor of New Testament,
> Trinity Evangelical Divinity School

"This book provides an excellent and much-needed focus on the individual church member. We can all benefit from this insightful book."
—R. C. SPROUL, Chairman and President,
Ligonier Ministries; Senior Minister of Preaching and
Teaching, Saint Andrews Chapel, Sanford, Florida

"A faithful pastor is also a good church member. Thabiti is evidence of this truth and thus has written with pastoral insight and personal experience on what it means to be a healthy church member. Any church desiring to strengthen its membership would do well to get this book into the hands of its members. Being a faithful church member in an age of overindulgence and selfish impulses is not easy. Yet, Thabiti not only reminds us it is possible, but he also challenges us with the biblical reality that it is necessary. I continue to thank God for the mind and heart of Thabiti Anyabwile."
—ANTHONY J. CARTER, pastor; author; editor,
*Experiencing the Truth: Bringing the Reformation
to the African-American Church*

"Thabiti Anyabwile's *What Is a Healthy Church Member?* asks the right questions about the offer of church membership, calling each local body of believers to cultivate and sustain practices of an assembly formed by the gospel. It is a most practical manual, yet it is free from the religious utilitarianism that often marks seeker-oriented works in this genre. Any leadership and laity that would elect to read this book together and embrace its exhortations would find their life as the family of God increasing in its wisdom, power, love, and witness in the world. What a balm we all will find in the words of this book!"
—ERIC C. REDMOND, Senior Pastor, Hillcrest Baptist
Church, Temple Hills, Maryland

WHAT IS A Healthy CHURCH MEMBER?

Thabiti M. Anyabwile

CROSSWAY

WHEATON, ILLINOIS

Cover design: Josh Dennis

Cover illustration: iStock

First printing 2008

Printed in the United States of America

Unless otherwise indicated, Scripture quotations are from the ESV® Bible (*The Holy Bible, English Standard Version®*), copyright © 2001 by Crossway. Used by permission. All rights reserved.

ISBN-13: 978-1-4335-0212-5
ISBN-10: 1-4335-0212-7
PDF ISBN: 978-1-4335-0456-3
Mobipocket ISBN: 978-1-4335-0457-0
ePub ISBN: 978-1-4335-2203-1

Library of Congress Cataloging-in-Publication Data
Anyabwile, Thabiti M., 1970–
 What is a healthy church member? / Thabiti M. Anyabwile;
foreword by Mark Dever.
  p. cm. — (IX marks series)
 ISBN 978-1-4335-0212-5 (hc)
 1. Church—Marks. I. Title.
BV601.A59   2008
248.4—dc22   2007051434

Crossway is a publishing ministry of Good News Publishers.

LB		23	22	21	20	19	18	17	16	15	14	13
21	20	19	18	17	16	15	14	13	12	11	10	9

For Jesus Christ, the Head of the church,
For his body and each member doing its part,
For local churches that have shaped me:

First Baptist Church of Grand Cayman,
Capitol Hill Baptist Church,
Church on the Rock

and

For the church that lives in my home:
Kristie, Afiya, Eden, and Titus

CONTENTS

SERIES PREFACE

The 9Marks series of books is premised on two basic ideas. First, the local church is far more important to the Christian life than many Christians today perhaps realize. A book called *What Is a Healthy Church Member?* might also be called *What Is a Healthy* Christian? We at 9Marks believe that a healthy Christian *is* a healthy church member.

Second, local churches grow in life and vitality as they organize their lives around God's Word. God speaks. Churches should listen and follow. It's that simple. When a church listens and follows, it begins to look like the One it is following. It reflects his love and holiness. It displays his glory. A church will look like him as it listens to him.

By this token, the reader might notice that all "9 marks," taken from Mark Dever's 2001 book, *Nine Marks of a Healthy Church* (Crossway Books), begin with the Bible:

- expositional preaching;
- biblical theology;
- a biblical understanding of the gospel;
- a biblical understanding of conversion;
- a biblical understanding of evangelism;
- a biblical understanding of church membership;
- a biblical understanding of church discipline;

- a biblical understanding of discipleship and growth; and
- a biblical understanding of church leadership.

More can be said about what churches should do in order to be healthy, such as pray. But these nine practices are the ones that we believe are most often overlooked today (unlike prayer). So our basic message to churches is, don't look to the best business practices or the latest styles; look to God. Start by listening to God's Word again.

Out of this overall project comes the 9Marks series of books. These volumes intend to examine the nine marks more closely and from different angles. Some target pastors. Some target church members. Hopefully all will combine careful biblical examination, theological reflection, cultural consideration, corporate application, and even a bit of individual exhortation. The best Christian books are always both theological and practical.

It's our prayer that God will use this volume and the others to help prepare his bride, the church, with radiance and splendor for the day of his coming.

FOREWORD

"Beloved." On Sunday mornings, that was the way Thabiti always greeted the congregation that we pastored together. And he meant it. He loved them, and they loved him. Some of the older members couldn't pronounce his name (*thuh-BEE-tee*), but they knew that Thabiti meant it when he called them "Beloved."

"Good morning, Beloved." I can still hear it.

That's also the word that the apostle John used again and again in his letters to some of the earliest churches. In God's providence, John's letters, together with the rest of the New Testament, tell us a lot about what it means to be Christians together. They tell us what it means to be a church member, which is what this little book is about, too.

Thabiti knows from experience that living the Christian life is not something that we're supposed to do alone. Being a Christian is a personal matter, not a private one. When you are born again, you are born into a family. And that family is not only the great extended family of Christians throughout the world, but also the particular nuclear family of a local congregation.

As a fellow church member for a number of years, I had the joy of knowing Thabiti and his wife, Kristie. I remember the first Sunday I met Thabiti. I was struck by how interesting (he worked at a "think tank"), how distinguished (he just looks the part), and how thoughtful (he was measured with his words) he was. But he wasn't simply a fascinating brain. The brother has a heart! He quickly began involving himself in the lives of other people in the church. Within a few weeks Thabiti was already helping to pastor the congregation. Though it would be several years before he was recognized as an elder, he was *eldering*.

All of this shows that Thabiti understands the idea that sheep are to be in a sheepfold, and I have seen him be both a great member of the sheepfold and an outstanding under-shepherd.

I've spent enough of your time now. This is supposed to be a short book. Now I invite you to jump into it and profit. But take a moment to pray before you do. Pray that God might use Thabiti in your life, as he has used him in so many other lives. Pray that God would use this book to help you know and love your local church in a way you never have before. And pray that, as you come to know and love your church, you would increasingly come to know and show God's love.

God bless and happy reading, Beloved.

Mark Dever,
Washington DC
September 2007

INTRODUCTION

Jenny surprised me when she started crying during our membership interview. The first twenty minutes of the interview were fairly routine. She recounted her childhood growing up in a Christian home, her high school years filled with fear, and a period of living as a prodigal during college. Then she recalled with some joy her conversion experience in a hometown local church.

So I did not expect her to sob at the question, "How was that church for you spiritually? Did you grow there?"

After pausing for a moment, she explained, "I expected that after my conversion someone would have helped me to grow as a Christian." She continued with a distinct trace of confusion and anger: "But it was as if people put me in a corner somewhere, as if they expected me to figure things out on my own. It was a terrible and lonely time."

How many Jennys have you met in your lifetime? Perhaps you are a Jenny. Perhaps you have spent considerable time in a local church, or several churches. And perhaps your Christian life is not too dissimilar from Jenny's. You came to the faith bright eyed and bushy tailed, bouncing with energy and zeal to do great things for the Lord. But soon you found yourself wondering, "What exactly am I supposed to be doing as a member of this local church?"

If so, this book is written for you. And if not, this book is written for you, too.

Whether your Christian life began yesterday or thirty years ago, the Lord's intent is that you play an active and vital part in his body, the local church. He intends for you to experience the local church as a home more profoundly wonderful and meaningful than any other place on earth. He intends for his churches to be healthy places and for the members of those churches to be healthy as well.

This little book is written in the hope that you might discover or rediscover what it means to be a healthy member of a local church, and what it means to contribute to the overall health of the church.

In 2007, Crossway Books published Mark Dever's *What Is a Healthy Church?* That book offered one definition of what a healthy church looks like biblically and historically and, along with his prior work *Nine Marks of a Healthy Church*, has shaped the thinking of many pastors and church leaders in the years since it was first published.

This book takes its cue from *What Is a Healthy Church?* though it attempts to answer a slightly different question: "What does a healthy church *member* look like in the light of Scripture?" While *Nine Marks of a Healthy Church* primarily addressed pastors in the task of church reform, this book seeks to address the people that pastors lead and to encourage those people to play their part in helping the local church to increasingly reflect the glory of God.

How can you, an individual member of a local church, contribute to the positive health of your church?

A lady named Mrs. Burns cornered me after the church

service one Sunday morning. She was a little hot and bothered about some of the things that were changing in the church as well as some of the things that were remaining the same. I tried to greet others as they were leaving while at the same time nodding politely to Mrs. Burns as she complained of her dissatisfaction.

When she paused in her litany, my first thought was to ask her, "So what exactly would you have me to do about these things?" But in a rare moment of insight I thought better of asking that question. Instead I asked her, "So what are *you* going to do about the state of the church? How will *you* become a better member and contribute to the health of God's family in this place?"

Those questions belong to every Christian, not just the ones who complain like Mrs. Burns. The health of the local church depends on the willingness of its members to inspect their hearts, correct their thinking, and apply their hands to the work of the ministry.

The chapters that follow present one proposal for becoming a healthier member of your local church. The chapters assume that you're already a member of a local congregation and that perhaps you just need a little nudge or the opportunity to think through a few key issues.[1]

Chapter 1 encourages "expositional listening" to the Word of God. Healthy church members are those who listen in a particular way to the Word of God as it is preached and studied—they let God set the agenda by seeking always to hear the true meaning of the text so that they can apply it to their lives.

In chapter 2, church members are encouraged to dedicate

themselves to learning the overarching themes of the Bible. In other words, they are asked to become "biblical theologians" in an effort to protect themselves and the church from false and unsound teaching.

Chapter 3 invites church members to be saturated in the gospel of Jesus Christ. It is the gospel that saves us (Rom. 1:16), and it is the gospel that will sustain and motivate us in our daily Christian lives.

There is no way to listen expositionally to the Scripture, to master its overarching narrative and themes, and to live a gospel-saturated life without also desiring and endeavoring to become a biblical evangelist. Chapters 4 and 5 offer some suggestions for thinking about conversion and evangelism in a biblically healthy way.

Chapter 6 is a call to make a serious and active commitment to membership in the local church. Then chapter 7 provides one reason why committed church membership is important: the local church is where Christians experience the shaping and correcting discipline of the Lord.

Chapter 8 examines spiritual growth from a biblical perspective, while chapter 9 includes some recommendations for effectively supporting the leadership of your local church.

Chapter 10 is a call to consider prayer an essential aspect of becoming and being a healthy church member. A brief discussion of the biblical basis of prayer is offered along with some suggested things for healthy church members to include in their prayer lives.

Each chapter also includes some recommended readings for further study. These are not the only things that make for a healthy church member; other things are important as well.

But I hope these stir us all to love and good deeds for the glory of Christ and the beauty of his bride.

> O Sovereign Lord, we beseech you to bless your people with an unusual humility, unity, joy, peace, and care for one another. We pray that you would increasingly make all of your people spiritually healthy and fruitful, not only as individuals but as one body, one new man, laboring together to grow up into Christ, even the fullness of his stature. Bless the reading, hearing, and study of your word for the glory of your name. And, O Lord, be pleased to use even this little book in some way to advance your kingdom and beautify your bride. Father, we ask these things knowing that nothing is too hard for you, with the full assurance of faith, in Jesus' name. Amen.

A HEALTHY CHURCH MEMBER IS AN EXPOSITIONAL LISTENER

What is "expositional listening"? Before answering that question, we need to define "expositional preaching." The first and most important mark of a healthy church is expositional preaching. "Expositional preaching is not simply producing a verbal commentary on some passage of Scripture. Rather, expositional preaching is that preaching which takes for the main point of a sermon the point of a particular passage of Scripture."[1] If churches are to be healthy, then pastors and teachers must be committed to discovering the meaning of Scripture and allowing that meaning to drive the agenda with their congregations.

There is an important corollary for every member of a local church. Just as the pastor's preaching agenda should be determined by the meaning of Scripture, so too should the Christian's listening agenda be driven by the meaning of Scripture. When we listen to the preaching of the Word, we should not listen primarily for "practical how-to advice," though Scripture teaches us much about everyday matters. Nor should we listen for messages that bolster our self-esteem or that rouse us to political and social causes. Rather, as members of Christian churches we should listen primarily for the voice and message of God as revealed in his Word. We should listen to hear what he has written, in his omniscient love, for his glory and for our blessing.

So what exactly do I mean by "expositional listening"? Expositional listening is listening for the meaning of a passage of Scripture and accepting that meaning as the main idea to be grasped for our personal and corporate lives as Christians.

What Are the Benefits of Expositional Listening?

Expositional listening benefits us, first, by *cultivating a hunger for God's Word*. As we tune our ears to the kind of preaching that makes the primary point of the sermon the primary point of a particular passage of Scripture, we grow accustomed to listening to God. We become fluent in the language of Zion and conversant with its themes. His Word, his voice, becomes sweet to us (Ps. 119:103–4); and as it does, we are better able to push to the background the many voices that rival God's voice for control over our lives. Expositional listening gives us a clear ear with which to hear God.

The second benefit follows from the first. Expositional listening *helps us to focus on God's will and to follow him*. Our agenda becomes secondary. The preacher's agenda becomes secondary. God's agenda for his people takes center stage, reorders our priorities, and directs us in the course that most honors him. The Lord himself proclaimed, "My sheep listen to my voice, and I know them, and they follow me" (John 10:27). Listening to the voice of Jesus as it is heard in his Word is critical to following him.

Third, expositional listening *protects the gospel and our lives from corruption*. The Scripture tells us "the time is coming when people will not endure sound teaching, but having itching ears they will accumulate for themselves teachers to suit their own passions, and will turn away from listening to the truth and wander off into myths" (2 Tim. 4:3–4). The failure to listen expositionally has disastrous effects. False teachers enter the church and hinder the gospel. Ultimately, the truth is displaced by myths and falsehoods. Where members cultivate the habit of expositional listening they guard themselves against "itching ears" and protect the gospel from corruption.

The fourth benefit, then, is that expositional listening *encourages faithful pastors*. Those men who serve faithfully in the ministry of the Word are worthy of double honor (1 Tim. 5:17). Few things are more discouraging or dishonoring to such men than a congregation inattentive to the Word of God. Faithful men flourish at the fertile reception of the preached Word. They're made all the more bold when their people give ear to the Lord's voice and give evidence of being shaped by it. As church members, we can care for our pastors and teachers and help to prevent unnecessary discouragement and fatigue by cultivating the habit of expositional listening.

Fifth, expositional listening *benefits the gathered congregation*. Repeatedly, the New Testament writers exhort local churches to be unified—to be of one mind. Paul writes to one local church, "I appeal to you, brothers, by the name of our Lord Jesus Christ, that all of you agree and that there may be no divisions among you, but that you may be united in the same mind and the same judgment" (1 Cor. 1:10; see also

Rom. 12:16; 2 Cor. 13:11; 1 Pet. 3:8). As we gather together in our local churches and give ourselves to hearing the voice of God through his preached Word, we're shaped into one body. We are united in understanding and purpose. And that unity testifies to the truth of the gospel of Jesus Christ (John 17:21). But if we listen with our own interests and agendas in mind, if we develop "private interpretations" and idiosyncratic views, we risk shattering that unity, provoking disputes over doubtful matters, and weakening our corporate gospel witness.

How Can Church Members Cultivate the Habit of Expositional Listening?

Well, if expositional listening is so vital to the health of individual church members and the church as a whole, how does a person form such a habit? At least six practical ideas can foster more attentive listening to God's word.

1) MEDITATE ON THE SERMON PASSAGE DURING YOUR QUIET TIME

Several days before the sermon is preached, ask the pastor what passage of Scripture he plans to preach the following Sunday. Encourage him by letting him know that you'll be praying for his preparation and preparing to listen to the sermon. Outline the text in your own daily devotions and use it to inform your prayer life. Learning to outline Scripture is a wonderful way of digging out and exposing the meaning of a passage. You can then use your outline as a listening aid; compare it to the preacher's outline for new insights you missed in your own study.

2) INVEST IN A GOOD SET OF COMMENTARIES

Add to your quiet times some of the greatest minds in Christian history. Study the Bible with John Calvin or Martin Lloyd-Jones by purchasing commentaries on books of the Bible as you read and study through them. If your pastor is preaching through John's Gospel, pick up D. A. Carson's or James Montgomery Boice's commentary on John. Let these scholars and pastors help you hear God's Word with a clear ear and discover its rich meaning. *The Bible Speaks Today* commentary series is an excellent starting place for those wanting to build a library of good commentaries. Also, you might want to purchase an Old Testament and New Testament commentary survey to help you sort through the range of commentary options available. Tremper Longman's *Old Testament Commentary Survey* and D. A. Carson's *New Testament Commentary Survey* are excellent resources.

3) TALK AND PRAY WITH FRIENDS ABOUT THE SERMON AFTER CHURCH

Instead of rushing off after the service is over, or talking about the latest news, develop the habit of talking about the sermon with people after church. Start spiritual conversations by asking, "How did the Scripture challenge or speak to you today?" Or, "What about God's character most surprised or encouraged you?" Encourage others by sharing things you learned about God and his Word during the sermon. Make particular note of how your thinking has changed because of the meaning of Scripture itself. And pray with others that God would keep the congregation from becoming "dull of hearing" and that he would bless the congregation with an increasingly strong desire for the "solid food" of his Word (Isa. 6:9–10; Heb. 5:11–14).

4) LISTEN TO AND ACT ON THE SERMON THROUGHOUT THE WEEK

We can cultivate the habit of expositional listening by listening to the sermon throughout the week and then acting upon it. Don't let the Sunday sermon become a one-time event that fades from memory as soon as it is over (James 1:22–25). Choose one or two particular applications from the Scripture and prayerfully put them into practice over the coming week. If your church has an audio ministry or a website that posts recent summaries, take advantage of these opportunities to feed your soul with the click of a mouse. With your pastor's support, establish small groups that review and apply the sermons. Or, use the sermons and your notes as a resource in one-on-one discipleship relationships. I know of several families that have a regular sermon-review time as their Sunday evening family devotional. There are a hundred ways to keep the sermon alive in your spiritual life by reviewing God's Word throughout the week. Be creative. It's well worth the planning.

5) DEVELOP THE HABIT OF ADDRESSING ANY QUESTIONS ABOUT THE TEXT ITSELF

Jonathan Edwards resolved that he would never let a day end before he had answered any questions that troubled him or sprang to mind while he was studying the Scripture.[2] How healthy would our churches be if members dedicated themselves to studying the Scripture with that kind of intentional effort and resolve? One way to begin is to follow up with your pastor, elders, or other teachers in the church about questions triggered by the text. Moreover, don't be passive in your private study; seek answers by searching the Scripture yourself and by talking with accountability partners or small groups. But don't forget that the pastor has likely spent more time than most in thinking about that passage and is there to feed you God's Word. Follow up the sermon with questions and comments that would be an encouragement to your pastor and a blessing to your soul.

6) CULTIVATE HUMILITY

As you dig into God's Word, listening for his voice, you will no doubt begin to grow and discover many wonderful treasures. But as you grow, do not become a "professional sermon listener" who is always hearing but never learning. Beware of false knowledge that "puffs up" (1 Cor. 8:1; Col. 2:18) and tends to cause strife and dissension. Mortify any tendencies toward pride, the condemnation of others, and critical nitpicking. Instead, seek to meet Jesus each time you come to the Scripture; gather from the Word fuel for all-of-life worship. Instead of exalting ourselves, let us remember the apostle Peter's words: "Humble yourselves, therefore, under God's mighty hand, that he may lift you up in due time" (1 Pet. 5:6).

Conclusion

It is hearing the message and the Word of God that leads to saving faith (Rom.10:17). Church members are healthy when they give themselves to hearing this message as a regular discipline. Expositional listening promotes such health for individual members and entire churches.

For Further Reflection

1. How would you rate your ability to listen for the meaning of the Word during private devotions? During sermons?

2. How do you plan to strengthen your listening ability?

A HEALTHY CHURCH MEMBER IS A BIBLICAL THEOLOGIAN

Ignorance of God—ignorance both of His ways and of the practice of communion with Him—lies at the root of the church's weakness today." That's how J. I. Packer began the 1973 preface to his classic volume *Knowing God.* Packer reasoned that one trend producing such ignorance of God and weakness in the church was "that Christian minds have been conformed to the modern spirit: the spirit, that is, that spawns great thoughts of man and leaves room for only small thoughts of God."[1]

Sadly, Packer's observation rings true more than three decades later. Ignorance of the ways of God and of communion with him is rampant in too many instances. Members of Christian churches continue to think small thoughts of God and great thoughts of man. This state of affairs reveals that too many Christians have neglected their first great calling: *to know their God.* Every Christian is meant to be a theologian in the best and most intimate sense of the word. If churches are to prosper in health, church members must be committed to being biblical theologians in whatever capacity they can. This is the second mark of a healthy church member.

What Is Biblical Theology for the Church Member?

To practice biblical theology is to know God himself. I'm using the term "biblical theology" with two things in mind. First, we must keep in mind that the Bible is the self-revelation of God; it is the source material for developing great thoughts about God. The Christian who is interested in knowing his God is the Christian who wants to know what God says about himself in the Bible. Such a Christian will not begin sentences with "I like to think of God as . . ." She has learned not to blend together a little New Age or a little Hinduism with a little Christianity in order to yield a custom-fitted deity for herself. No, the Christian church member who is serious about knowing God is the member who is committed to what the Bible says about God, because the Bible is where God tells us about himself.

To practice biblical theology is to know God's macro story of redemption. Second, the biblical theologian is a person committed to understanding the history of revelation, the grand themes and doctrines of the Bible, and how they fit together. In other words, healthy church members give themselves to understanding the unity and progression of the Bible as a whole—not just isolated or favorite passages. They approach the Bible knowing that they are reading one awesome story of God redeeming for himself a people for his own glory. And in that story, they see that God is a creating God, a holy God, a faithful God, a loving God, and a sovereign God as he makes and keeps his promises to his people, beginning with Adam and Eve and progressing to the final consummation of all things.[2]

How Does Biblical Theology Work to Promote Health in a Church Member?

In his popular *Systematic Theology*, Wayne Grudem outlines several benefits to studying systematics. Many of those benefits come with doing biblical theology as well. Grudem's proposed benefits are worth summarizing here.[3]

First, *practicing biblical theology helps us grow in our reverence for God.* As we encounter the God of Scripture who establishes and keeps his covenant promises with his people, we see something of God's majesty. The Lord's working of all things together for good comes into clearer focus, from his promise to the woman that her Seed would bruise the serpent's head (Gen. 3:15), to the opening of barren wombs so that the Seed would be preserved (Gen. 17:15–19; 21:1–2; 29:31; 30:22; Isa. 7:14), to the actual birth of that Seed (Matt. 1:20–23). When we see that God is, always has been, and always will be the same creating, holy, faithful, loving, and sovereign God for us that he has been for others, we are stirred to faith and awe in God. If we want to know and reverence God truly, we will dedicate ourselves to becoming biblical theologians who understand the narrative and themes of Scripture.

Second, *practicing biblical theology helps us to overcome our wrong ideas.* All of us encounter various teachings in the Bible that challenge, confuse, or provoke us. Often, we refuse to accept these teachings because of dullness and sin in our hearts. We can evade one verse here or there that displeases or confronts us. But when we give ourselves to understanding the grand sweep of biblical revelation and the total weight of Scripture's teaching on a particular subject, we are more readily convinced of our wrong ideas. Biblical theology helps us to see how God has consistently spoken the same message to his people in diverse places and diverse ways (Heb. 1:1), a message that we will all one day bow to and accept (Isa. 45:22–24; Rom. 14:10–12; Phil. 2:9–11). As we prayerfully study biblical theology, we're led to joyfully submit to God and to jettison our wrong ideas about him.

Third, *practicing biblical theology helps inoculate the church against doctrinal controversies.* Church history is replete with controversies rising within and between congregations. Churches are better able to withstand and productively resolve such controversies when they maintain a good understanding of biblical, systematic, and historical theology. This is true because whatever the Bible has to say about one thing is related to everything else the Bible says. Biblical theology helps to maintain the continuity and consistency of the Bible's teaching. Engaging in biblical theology is akin to putting together a jigsaw puzzle. When one piece of the puzzle appears unfamiliar, we can search for its proper place in the puzzle by relating it to the bigger picture on the puzzle box. The more pieces we have in place to begin with, the easier it is to evaluate and fit in new pieces and the less apt we are to make mistakes. Adequately grasping biblical theology is much like having the picture of the completed puzzle, allowing us to accept or reject errant theological pieces. The Scriptures "were written down as warnings for us, on whom the fulfillment of the ages has come" (1 Cor. 10:11), and knowledge of Scripture protects the church from clever wives' tales and endless disputes.

Fourth, *the practice of biblical theology is necessary to fulfilling the Great Commission.* Jesus commands us to teach all believers to observe all that he commands (Matt. 28:19–20). Without a well-formed theology, including an accurate understanding of how God's commands are to be understood in their historical development and context, it is difficult indeed to obey the Lord's command to teach others to obey. What shall we teach? What shall we obey? How shall we know what to apply to our lives? These questions are better answered when Christians are knowledgeable of biblical theology and know their God.

But perhaps the most compelling benefit for doing biblical theology is that it *deepens our understanding of and facility with the gospel.* Jesus and the apostles did not need the New Testament to proclaim the gospel. They relied on the Old Testament and understood that the Old Testament Scriptures pointed to Jesus (Luke 24:27, 44–45). The biblical theologian follows in the steps of Jesus and the apostles by mastering the unity of Scripture, seeing Christ and the gospel throughout.

How to Become a Healthy Church Member by Becoming a Biblical Theologian

How can a Christian become a healthy church member conversant with the themes of biblical theology? Several strategies may be helpful.

READ A GOOD BOOK ON BIBLICAL THEOLOGY

One obvious way to become a biblical theologian is to read a good book on biblical theology. Several works have proven useful over the years. For a good reference work, readers should try *The New Dictionary of Biblical Theology.*[4] For helpful introductions consider:

- Vaughn Roberts, *God's Big Picture: Tracing the Storyline of the Bible*;
- Mark Strom, *The Symphony of Scripture: Making Sense of the Bible's Many Themes*;
- Peter Jensen, *At the Heart of the Universe: What Christians Believe*;
- Graeme Goldsworthy, *According to Plan: The Unfolding Revelation of God in the Bible*; and
- Graeme Goldsworthy, *The Goldsworthy Trilogy: Gospel and Kingdom, Gospel and Wisdom, and The Gospel in Revelation.*[5]

The New Studies in Biblical Theology[6] series edited by D. A. Carson provides an excellent series of studies in biblical theology. These works provide solid and readable overviews of the unity and diversity of Scripture. And for more advanced readers, Dutch-born Princeton theologian Geerhardus Vos's *Biblical Theology: Old and New Testaments*[7] is still a classic. Use these works in your devotional or free reading times. Suggest to your small-group leader that you read one or more works like these as a group.

STUDY THE SCRIPTURES THEMATICALLY

Allot some portion of your private devotions to *study the Scriptures thematically*. The main diet of Scripture intake should probably be a study of books of the Bible verse-by-verse in their redemptive historical context. Supplement this main diet with a study of major themes that run throughout the Bible. Spend some time considering the revelation of the character of God; the unity and diversity of the covenant of God with his people; the prophethood, priesthood, and kingship of Jesus; and the kingdom of God in both the Old and

New Testaments. Trace these themes throughout Scripture and make note of the continuities and discontinuities across various periods of redemptive history. As you do this, the excellencies of God and the glories of redemption will come into view in a more nuanced and brilliant way.

ADOPT THE NEW TESTAMENT'S ATTITUDE TOWARD THE OLD TESTAMENT

As we stated earlier, the Bible is one story about God's redeeming for himself a special people. When studying the New Testament, train yourself to link what you learn there to the Old Testament. Ask questions like these:

- How is this passage a fulfillment of something promised in the Old Testament?
- How is this New Testament idea different from or similar to an Old Testament teaching?
- In what way does this New Testament passage clarify, unveil, or amplify something from the Old Testament?

Asking these questions will help to underscore the unity and diversity of the Bible and its message. An excellent book to study with these questions in mind is the book of Hebrews. Study Hebrews and be amazed at the supremacy of Jesus Christ demonstrated in the Old Testament.

STUDY THE OLD TESTAMENT WITH JESUS AND THE NEW TESTAMENT IN VIEW

As you read and study the Old Testament, ask yourself how it fits together with the revelation of the New Testament. For example, ask:

- Where does this passage fit in the time line of redemptive history?
- How does this passage point us to Jesus?
- How does this truth about Israel relate to the New Testament idea of the church?
- How is this passage foundational for an understanding of New Testament Christianity? How is this idea or teaching in the Old Testament continuous or discontinuous with the New Testament?
- Which New Testament passages help me to answer these questions?

A student of biblical theology is well versed in the continuing drama of Scripture.

STUDY THE BOOKS OF PROPHECY IN THE OLD TESTAMENT

Perhaps the most neglected books of the Old Testament are the books of prophecy, especially the unfortunately named "Minor Prophets." The prophets contain some of the richest material in Scripture about the life, ministry, and supremacy of Jesus Christ. As you study Isaiah or Zechariah, for example, remember that their prophecies could be fulfilled on multiple horizons. Any given prophecy could have been fulfilled, in one respect, in the prophet's own day. The same prophecy could also be "christologically" fulfilled in Jesus Christ. And then it could be "eschatologically" fulfilled, that is, occurring at the end of time in the consummation of all things. Studying and understanding prophecy in this way helps to emphasize the big picture of the Bible and to deepen our knowledge of God.

KNOW AND AGREE TO SUPPORT YOUR CHURCH'S STATEMENT OF FAITH

When we join a church, we should know what the church believes and whether we agree with its teaching. Therefore, commit yourself to studying the church's statement of faith. Is it doctrinally sound? Is it a statement with a special history in that local church? Does the statement of faith agree with or depart from the broader Christian tradition? Do you understand the statement? Some churches have a healthy practice of requiring new members to sign the church's statement of faith as an indication of their agreement with and willingness to defend the truths expressed therein. Could you in good conscience sign your church's statement of faith? If so, commit yourselves to upholding the doctrinal integrity of your church.

SEEK DOCTRINAL UNITY AND AVOID NEEDLESS DISPUTES

From time to time, doctrinal differences will arise in a local church. The key question for members is, "How will you participate in the resolution of such differences?" The old maxim is useful here: "In all things essential, unity; in all things nonessential, liberty; and in all things, love." A healthy church member, committed to becoming a biblical theologian, will work to know the difference between beliefs that are essential to biblical Christianity and beliefs that are nonessential to the integrity and continuance of the faith. Healthy church members will commit themselves to defending the essential things of the gospel (Phil. 1:27; Jude 3), while avoiding strife and contention over things that are not essential to the gospel. The apostle Paul's instructions to Timothy are appropriate:

Remind them of these things, and charge them before God not to quarrel about words, which does no good, but only ruins the hearers. Do your best to present yourself to God as one approved, a worker who has no need to be ashamed, rightly handling the word of truth. But avoid irreverent babble, for it will lead people into more and more ungodliness, and their talk will spread like gangrene. (2 Tim. 2:14–17a)

On the one hand, we are to be workmen who are skilled in correctly handling the word of truth; on the other hand, we must be innocent of engendering disagreements over things of no value. Quarreling about petty and inconsequential things "only ruins those who listen" and, like a gangrenous growth, leads to more and more ungodliness. Let us work for unity in belief and peace in our churches, remembering that "it is an honor for a man to keep aloof from strife, but every fool will be quarreling" (Prov. 20:3).

Conclusion

According to J. I. Packer, knowing God starts with knowing about him, about his character. It also involves giving yourself to God based upon his promise to be your God through repentance and faith in Jesus Christ, his Son. Consequently, knowing God means following Jesus as a disciple. And, ultimately, knowing God means being "more than a conqueror" by exulting in the adequacy of God in all things. Such knowledge of God comes only from drinking deeply from the message of the Bible with all of its rich themes. And such knowledge of God belongs especially to those Christian church members who commit to becoming biblical theologians.

For Further Reflection

1. How familiar are you with biblical theology? Do you think you have an adequate grasp of the major themes and developments of the Bible? Could you explain to a new Christian or a non-Christian how the entire Bible fits together as one book?

2. What specific plans could you make to strengthen your knowledge of biblical theology?

A HEALTHY CHURCH MEMBER IS GOSPEL SATURATED

The greatest need in the world today is the gospel. It is the greatest need of the world because men, women, and children are perishing without a vital knowledge of God through the good news of our Savior and his Son, Jesus.

The greatest need in the church today is the gospel. The gospel is not only news for a perishing world, it is the message that forms, sustains, and animates the church. Apart from the gospel, the church has nothing to say—that is, nothing to say that cannot be said by some other human agency. The gospel distinguishes the church from the world, defines her message and mission in the world, and steels her people against the fiery darts of the evil one and the false allurements of sin. The gospel is absolutely vital to a vibrant, joyous, persevering, hopeful, and healthy Christian and Christian church. So essential is the gospel to the Christian life that we need to be *saturated* in it in order to be healthy church members.

Becoming Gospel Saturated

How then do we immerse ourselves in the gospel? What path might lead to greater spiritual health?

KNOW THE GOSPEL

The first order of business is to know the gospel. This seems so obvious that stating it can feel silly. But, in point of fact, many professing and believing Christians possess a shallow understanding of the gospel as a result of years of hearing short "gospel presentations" tacked onto the ends of sermons. Still others who know the message of Christ find themselves feeling awkward and incapable of sharing the good news clearly with family and friends. Taking steps to be sure we know the gospel with some clarity and depth, then, is necessary.

It's helpful to rule out some ideas frequently presented as the gospel. The gospel is *not* simply that (a) we are okay, (b) that God is love, (c) that Jesus wants to be our friends, or (d) that we should live right.[1] Neither is the gospel simply that all our problems will be fixed if we follow Jesus, or that God wants us to be healthy, wealthy, and wise. All of these ideas may be true in some sense, but only in a partial sense and never as a solely sufficient statement of what the gospel is.

The gospel of Jesus Christ is literally "good news." As *news* it contains statements of fact and truths derived from those facts. As *good* news the gospel holds out hope based upon promises of God and grounded in the historical facts and truths that vindicate those promises.

The gospel or good news of Jesus Christ is that God the Father, who is holy and righteous in all his ways, is angry with sinners and will punish sin. Man, who disobeys the rule of God, is alienated from the love of God and is in danger of an eternal and agonizing condemnation at the hands of God. But God, who is also rich in mercy, because of his great love, sent his eternal Son born by the Virgin Mary, to die as a ransom and a substitute for the sins of rebellious people. And now, through the perfect obedience of the Son of God and his willing death on the cross as payment for our sins, all who repent and believe in Jesus Christ, following him as Savior and Lord, will be saved from the wrath of God to come, be declared just in his sight, have eternal life, and receive the Spirit of God as a foretaste of the glories of heaven with God himself.

It is this message—briefly stated here—that we must imbibe and delight in if we are to be healthy church members.

DESIRE TO HEAR THE GOSPEL AND PREACH THE GOSPEL TO YOURSELF

We must cultivate and protect a ravenous desire for this message. Regularly hearing and plumbing the depths of the gospel increases our knowledge of the message, our affection for the Savior, and our skill in sharing the message.

So we should listen actively for the gospel and gospel implications in sermons. Don't turn off your ears when the pastor begins to appeal to non-Christians with the gospel message. Listen to it afresh. Reaffirm your belief in its truth, promises, and power in your life. Appropriate it for any sins that you become conscious of through the sermon or self-examination. See *your* sins nailed to the cross as you hear the good news. Consider whether there are any new promises or aspects to the gospel included in the sermon. How will you hold onto those truths?

Listen so actively and longingly for this news that you feel your poverty and malnourishment when it's missing in a sermon. And when you find yourself dissatisfied or longing, preach the gospel to yourself. It's a message that comes to you, for you. Own it. Rather than merely listening to others, or listening to that voice that plagues you with doubts, worries, and fears, listen to the voice of God in the gospel by proclaiming it to yourself when the need arises. C. J. Mahaney, in his excellent and helpful book *Living the Cross Centered Life: Keeping the Gospel the Main Thing,* suggests that we memorize the gospel, pray the gospel, sing the gospel, review how the gospel has changed us, and study the gospel.

TAKE THE GOSPEL TO ITS CONCLUSION

As you reflect on the events and promises of the gospel, press forward to the conclusion of the gospel. John Piper reminds us that God is the gospel, that the gospel is a message about God giving himself to us in love:

> Until the gospel **events** of Good Friday and Easter and the gospel **promises** of justification and eternal life lead you to behold and embrace **God himself** as your highest joy, you have not embraced the gospel of God. You have embraced some of his gifts. You have rejoiced over some of his rewards. You have marveled at some of his miracles. But you have not yet been awakened to why the gifts, the rewards, and the miracles have come. They have come for one great reason: that you might behold forever the glory of God in Christ, and by beholding become the kind of person who delights in God above all things, and by delighting display his supreme beauty and worth with ever-increasing brightness and bliss forever.[2]

ORDER YOUR LIFE AROUND THE GOSPEL

As church members, our aim is to understand the gospel so deeply, so intimately, that it animates every area of our lives.

We want the gospel central to our communication with others, central to how we encourage and correct, central to individual career and relationship decisions, central to the decisions the church makes corporately, and central to all our habits of life. We want the gospel, the God of the gospel, to take priority in every area of life. Gospel-saturated church members should consider any number of strategies for organizing their lives around the good news of Jesus Christ:

- intentionally frequenting the same stores (cleaners, restaurants, etc.) with the aim of building relationships and familiarity with store personnel, and hopefully having gospel conversations;
- using vacations for short-term mission trips;
- volunteering in community organizations to influence for the gospel;
- hosting home discussions regarding religion and philosophy;
- inviting neighbors over for dinner or for holiday parties and talking with them about Christ;
- hosting Bible studies in the work place;
- joining neighborhood clubs (garden clubs, cycling clubs, etc.) to build relationships and further gospel opportunities;
- inviting friends to church and special religious events where the gospel is sure to be center stage.

We want to recognize that there is no risk in sharing the gospel, only the reward of faithfulness. We want to be "at the ready" with the words of life.

SHARE THE GOSPEL WITH OTHERS

It sometimes appears as though some Christians believe the gospel was meant to be preached widely until it reached them and then stored safely in the vault of their personal history, away from everyone else. Christians can suppose that just sharing their testimony or living a good Christian life is as effective a witness as doing evangelism. No doubt such a life is a witness of sorts. But is it a witness to the cross of Jesus Christ? Does "witnessing" through our personal testimonies and good deeds point effectively enough to the cross and the Savior?

In too many cases such attempts leave only a vague impression of religiosity, not a brilliant display of the glories of God in the redemption of sinners through the sacrifice of his Son. If we would contribute to the health of our local congregations, we must be committed not only to harvesting the gospel for ourselves but to shipping it to others as well. We must do the work of an evangelist. With urgency and love we must tell the non-Christians among us to repent of their sins and to believe on Jesus Christ. We must tell them that turning to God does not result in an easy life, but the decision is well worth it. The forgiveness and satisfaction their souls long for is found only in the person of Jesus Christ.

We have an opportunity to improve the work of our pastor by planting and watering gospel seeds even as he plants and waters through his pulpit ministry. We can greet and talk with visitors to our churches and invite our non-Christian family and friends. We should use the occasion of their visit to discuss spiritual things, particularly their understanding of and their acceptance or rejection of the good news. We can meet together with other Christians specifically to plot and pray for evangelistic opportunities. A gospel-saturated life is a life that splashes out onto others with the good news. A healthy church is built, in part, on healthy gospel-motivated members.

GUARD THE GOSPEL

Finally, a healthy church member takes seriously the responsibility of guarding the gospel from corruption and abandonment. The New Testament seems to place this responsibility ultimately on the congregation rather than on the pastors alone. When the churches at Galatia were unsettled by false teachers who were trying to add circumcision to the demands of the gospel, the apostle Paul wrote not to the pastors and elders but to the churches themselves. He addressed the membership and called them to guard the gospel he had preached to them. His instruction is strong:

> But even if we or an angel from heaven should preach to you a gospel contrary to the one we preached to you, let him be accursed. As we have said before, so now I say again: If anybody is preaching to you a gospel contrary to the one you received, let him be eternally accursed. (Gal. 1:8–9)

The Galatians, indeed all Christian church members, are to be careful concerning what they entertain in gospel preaching. The apostle John warns his readers that "if anyone comes to you and does not bring this teaching, do not receive him into your house or give him any greeting, for whoever greets him takes part in his wicked work" (2 John 10–11). Peter reminds his readers that those who follow the "shameful ways" of false teachers cause "the way of truth to be blasphemed" (2 Pet. 2:2). So it's understandable, then, that Jude exhorts his audience to "*contend* for the faith that was once for all delivered to the saints" (Jude 3). The healthy church and church member fight for and protect the apostolic gospel delivered and preserved in the pages of Scripture. When we don't accept that responsibility and are not vigilant in understanding and applying the gospel, we leave it to be corrupted, abused, and abandoned by unscrupulous teachers and the forces of the evil one.

Conclusion

In the gospel of Jesus Christ, God offers himself for sinners and to sinners. It is the gospel that makes us aware of the love of God, of our depravity and need for redemption, and of the possibility of eternal joy through worshiping God. It is this same gospel, and a healthy understanding of it, that creates health and strength in members of the Christian church. Let us be saturated in it!

For Further Reflection

What strategies will you put into place to keep yourself thinking about, applying, and sharing the gospel?

For Further Reading

Bridges, Jerry. *The Gospel for Real Life*. Colorado Springs, CO: NavPress, 2003.

——. *The Discipline of Grace*. Colorado Springs, CO: NavPress, 1994.

Mahaney, C. J. *Living the Cross Centered Life: Keeping the Gospel the Main Thing*. Sisters, OR: Multnomah, 2006.

Piper, John. *God Is the Gospel: Meditations on God's Love as the Gift of Himself*. Wheaton, IL: Crossway, 2005.

Spurgeon, Charles. *The Power of the Cross of Christ*. Seattle, WA: YWAM Publishing, 1996.

Stott, John. *The Cross of Christ*. Downers Grove, IL: Intervarsity, 2006 (twentieth anniversary edition).

A HEALTHY CHURCH MEMBER IS GENUINELY CONVERTED

My friend Curtis possesses a contagious Christian joy. He loves the Lord and is zealous in evangelism. Curtis's zeal is marked by a willingness to "do whatever it takes" to have someone "profess faith in Christ."

One day Curtis, with his usual joy, told me of a mutual friend, Kenny, who "got born again." I was struck by Curtis's choice of words. Pressing past his excitement, I asked, "How do you know he was 'born again'?"

Curtis withdrew slightly, head tilting with the curiosity puppies sometimes display at odd human behavior, "What do you mean?"

"Well, how can you be so confident that spiritual rebirth occurred?"

Relief washed over Curtis's face and shoulders. "Oh. That's easy. He came down front after the service and prayed to receive Christ—the way lots of people get saved."

About a year after my conversation with Curtis, he telephoned, quite concerned. A problem that periodically troubled him was again causing him discomfort—only this time it was our friend Kenny. Curtis told me how Kenny began the Christian race well, attending public services, praying fervently, going out with evangelism teams, and sometimes showing great emotion during public services. "The first year was great," Curtis reported. "But then," his voice quieting, "Kenny just faded away. It's like he just petered out . . . and now he's having marital problems and considering leaving the faith."

Silence occupied the phone line for a moment. Then Curtis asked, "Do you think Kenny was ever really saved? How can you tell if someone is born again?"

Getting Conversion Correct

As we're thinking through a list of things a healthy church member must be, a good case can be made for beginning right here—with the fact that a healthy church member must be genuinely converted. The healthy church member—the true church member—must know the work of God's grace in his or her own soul. We must be converted ourselves. This may sound obvious, but probably 40 percent of the people I interview for membership in our local church tell me of a time when they were church members but did not understand the gospel and were not, by their own assessment, converted people. The experience is widespread. Even famous Christians like John Wesley tell such a story.

Understanding Biblical Conversion

Surely one of the reasons for the vast number of nominal Christians—those who hold to the faith in name only—in the history of the Christian church is that churches have failed to embrace and teach a biblical understanding of conversion. If we want to understand conversion rightly, we must begin with the Bible's diagnosis of fallen man. To apply the proper treatment and cure, we must recognize the illness.

All men suffer the illness of sin. Not only do men sin, but men are sinners by nature (Eph. 2:1–3). At his root, his core, his heart, man is alienated from and hostile toward God. He prefers to satisfy his sinful cravings and desires more than to honor and worship God—so much so that he is a slave to sin.

> For those who live according to the flesh set their minds on the things of the flesh, but those who live according to the Spirit set their minds on the things of the Spirit. To set the mind on the flesh is death, but to set the mind on the Spirit is life and peace. For the mind that is set on the flesh is hostile to God, for it does not submit to God's law; indeed, it cannot. Those who are in the flesh cannot please God. (Rom. 8:5–8)

Because man is a sinner by nature, he is guilty before God and deserves the punishment God promises. Unless there is a radical and profound change in his spiritual condition, man is doomed to judgment. With his mind set on evil, he cannot and does not even desire to please God. He desperately needs to be changed. He needs a new heart.

This radical change is what Christian theology calls "conversion." Conversion is the radical turn from an enslaved life of pursuing sin to a free life of pursuing and worshiping God. Conversion is a change of life, not merely a decision. This change is not a matter of moral rectitude, self help, or mere behavior modification. It is not accomplished by outward displays or religious practices like "walking the aisle." It cannot be accomplished by human effort but only by the power of God.

Conversion is a change so dramatic that it requires the intervention of God the Holy Spirit. In conversion the Spirit of God grants the twin graces of repentance and faith to sinners who turn from sin and turn to God through faith in Jesus Christ.[1] The New Hampshire Confession of Faith's eighth article defines biblical conversion well:

> We believe that Repentance and Faith are sacred duties, and also inseparable graces, wrought in our souls by the regenerating Spirit of God; whereby being deeply convinced of our guilt, danger and helplessness, and of the way of salvation by Christ, we turn to God with unfeigned contrition, confession, and supplication for mercy; at the same time heartily receiving the Lord Jesus Christ as our Prophet, Priest, and King, and relying on Him alone as the only and all sufficient Saviour.

Conversion, then, requires genuine conviction of sin that leads to turning around (repentance) and relying only on the Lord Jesus Christ for salvation (faith).

Knowing Our Own Souls

How then will a biblical understanding of conversion affect what we do in our churches practically? It's worth thinking about both the inward and the outward implications.

So start by looking inward. We need to ask ourselves if we have received a changed heart by God's grace through faith in Jesus Christ. This sort of self-examination is a spiritually healthy thing to do. In fact, this is what the apostles often exhorted their readers to do (2 Cor. 13:5; Phil. 2:12; 2 Pet. 1:5–11). The first order of business is to know our own souls. Are we trusting in the finished work of Christ alone for our salvation? Is there evidence of God's grace in our lives? Are we growing in the grace and knowledge of Jesus Christ, in the fruit of the Spirit (Gal. 5:22–24), and in the virtues mentioned in Christ's beatitudes (Matt. 5:3–12)?

The book of 1 John is a helpful book to study when examining the work of God in our souls. John offers several tests to help Christians know if they have savingly come to faith in Christ. In an effort to know our soul's standing before God, we might examine ourselves with the following proofs.

DO WE WALK IN THE LIGHT OR THE DARKNESS?

"If we say we have fellowship with him while we walk in darkness, we lie and do not practice the truth. But if we walk in the light, as he is in the light, we have fellowship with one another, and the blood of Jesus his Son cleanses us from all sin" (1 John 1:6–7). Genuine converts to Christ grieve at their sin. They hate their sins, and they desire the light of life in Christ, which is to say they desire and work to walk in integrity and righteousness. Persons habitually and unrepentantly living in sin, who deny that they are sinners (vv. 8–10), are not genuinely converted. "No one who abides in him keeps on sinning; no one who keeps on sinning has either seen him or known him" (1 John 3:5).

DO WE LOVE GOD THE FATHER?

Some people appear to love Jesus "meek and mild" but show no affection for God the Father, whom they reckon to be the unloving God of the Old Testament. Thinking of Jesus as a God of love and tolerance allows some people to believe that God will not judge sin or condemn the sinner. They may view God the Father as an Old Testament tyrant and reject the Bible's teaching about God because they find it out-of-date, unsatisfying, or repulsive. But the apostle John makes love for the Father a test of genuine faith. "Do not love the world or the things in the world. If anyone loves the world, the love of the Father is not in him" (1 John 2:15). "Who is the liar but he who denies that Jesus is the Christ? This is the antichrist, he who denies the Father and the Son. No one who denies the Son has the Father. Whoever confesses the Son has the Father also" (1 John 2:22–23). There is but one God—Father, Son, and Holy Spirit. There is no way to love both the world and the Father. And there is no way to embrace Christ without embracing the Father, or to come to the Father without believing on Christ. Love for God the Father is a test of genuine conversion.

DO WE LOVE OTHER CHRISTIANS?

Many people appear to live without genuine affection or concern for other Christians. They think of the Christian walk as a "solo sport." However, "everyone who believes that Jesus is the Christ has been born of God, and everyone who loves the Father loves whoever has been born of him" (1 John 5:1). "Whoever does not love abides in death. Everyone who hates his brother is a murderer, and you know that no murderer has eternal life abiding in him" (1 John 3:14b–15). "Little children, let us not love in word or talk but in deed and in truth. By this we shall know that we are of the truth and reassure our heart before him" (1 John 3:18–19). John teaches that the commandment is to believe in the name of Jesus Christ and to love one another. If our love of other Christians is cold, we need to examine whether or not we have savingly believed on Christ Jesus the Son of God.

DO WE HAVE THE TESTIMONY OF THE SPIRIT THAT WE ARE CHILDREN OF GOD?

"And by this we know that he abides in us, by the Spirit whom he has given us" (1 John 3:24b). The Father has not left us without a testimony of his love. We may be assured of our adoption into his family by God himself, the Holy Spirit, assuring us. "And because you are sons, God has sent the Spirit of his Son into our hearts, crying, 'Abba, Father!'" (Gal. 4:6; see also Rom. 8:15). "The Spirit himself bears witness with our spirit that we are children of God" (Rom. 8:16). We know that we live in God and God in us because we received the Holy Spirit when we believed the gospel (1 John 4:13–14).

ARE WE PERSEVERING IN THE FAITH?

"For everyone who has been born of God overcomes the world. And this is the victory that has overcome the world— our faith. Who is it that overcomes the world except the one who believes that Jesus is the Son of God?" (1 John 5:4–5). Those who believe and continue to believe are those who overcome the world by faith in Christ. Genuine faith is a per-severing faith. This doesn't mean that hard things in life don't sometimes cause doubt or discomfort. But it does mean that the genuine Christian presses onward in faith, trusting God and his good plans and will. After all, the same Spirit whom the true believer receives also seals and keeps the believer until that day (Eph. 1:13–14; 1 Pet. 1:3–5).

Asking these kinds of questions is best done in the fellowship of the local church, among committed and growing Christians who can help us see ourselves accurately. Some people are given to an "easy believism" that resists careful curation of their own souls, while others are too easily tempted to doubt and despair. In a church culture, we can love each other both by pointing out evidence of God's grace in each others' lives and by asking tough questions about our profession and walk. By doing both, we help one another avoid the extremes of despair and complacency, and we encourage one another to see ourselves in the light of God's saving work in our souls.

Implications for Evangelism

In addition to looking inside (and helping others to do the same), we want to look outside, as it were, at our understanding of conversion and how it affects our church's approach to evangelism. When it comes to the work of evangelism, the healthy church member must properly understand who it is that actually converts the sinner; it is God the Holy Spirit. And the healthy church member must recognize, then, that evangelism is not a matter of clever technique but of relying on the Spirit of God to bless the Word of God to effect spiritual rebirth and the radical change of conversion. We'll consider biblical evangelism further in the next chapter.

Conclusion

Over the years I've lost touch with Kenny. I don't know if he is living a Christian life or if he has turned from the truth to the world. I do know that it is absolutely essential that he search himself to know whether he is in the faith. And I know that that search will only be fruitful if he looks to discover the proofs of conversion that God spells out in his Word.

For Further Reflection

With a group of mature Christian church members and friends, use the following questions to consider and cite evidence of God's grace among you and, if necessary, identify areas where grace is needed.

1. Do we walk in the light or in the darkness (1 John 1:6–7)?

2. Do we love God the Father or do we appear to love the world (1 John 2:15)?

3. Do we love other Christians (1 John 3:14–15, 18–19; 5:1)?

4. Do we have the testimony of the Holy Spirit that we are children of God (Rom. 8:15–16; Gal. 4:6; 1 John 3:24b)?

5. Are we persevering in the faith (1 John 5:4–5)?

For Further Reading

Dever, Mark E. *Nine Marks of a Healthy Church*. Wheaton, IL: Crossway Books, 2004 (see chap. 4).

Luther, Martin. *The Bondage of the Will*. Grand Rapids, MI: Baker Books, 1990.

Murray, John. *Redemption Accomplished and Applied*. Grand Rapids, MI: Eerdmans, 1984.

Smallman, Stephen. *What Is True Conversion?* Phillipsburg, NJ: P&R, 2005.

Whitney, Donald. *Ten Questions to Diagnose Your Spiritual Health*. Colorado Springs, CO: NavPress, 2002.

A HEALTHY CHURCH MEMBER IS A BIBLICAL EVANGELIST

In the last chapter, we discussed the important doctrine of conversion. We began that chapter with the story of Kenny, a friend who "made a profession of faith" but subsequently turned away from Christ.

What is painfully obvious now to my friend Curtis and me is that "the gospel presentation" that Kenny heard some years ago was the shallowest message possible. It was not a biblically faithful proclamation of (1) the holiness and righteousness of the sovereign God who created all things; (2) the sinfulness of man and the judgment due to him for rebelling against God; (3) the need of man for a radical change, for a new heart and perfect righteousness; (4) the fact that only Jesus Christ has provided the righteousness we need and made the atonement for our sins that satisfies God the Father; and (5) Kenny's need to bring forth fruit worthy of repentance and to rely solely on Christ Jesus.

I'm certain some of those things were presented to Kenny. But I'm also certain that biblical faithfulness required *more than what Curtis shared* and *more of Kenny than Curtis asked*. It's frightening to think about how many people have not tasted the goodness of God and his salvation, not because Christians have not had opportunity to share, but because we have been so shallow in what we did share. A healthy church member works to make sure that he himself is converted, but he also works to make sure that his evangelistic efforts are informed by a biblical understanding of conversion.

A Biblical Understanding of Evangelism

Apart from a biblical understanding of conversion and evangelism, a church member will be most unhelpful in completing the church's mission of making disciples. Yet with the contemporary church's fascination with pragmatic ("if it works, do it") methods and techniques, it is easy for members to be led in unhealthy directions if they don't understand conversion and evangelism. "Unprincipled pragmatism is in the end not only unfaithful, but also unpragmatic."[1]

The encouraging news is that when we have a good grasp of conversion, we realize that evangelism does not depend on eloquence, using the correct mood lighting, emotionally sappy stories and songs, or high-pressure sales pitches. We are free to simply and deeply trust God and the power of the gospel to produce the fruit he desires (Rom. 1:17). We realize that, though we are ambassadors for Christ pleading with men to be reconciled to God, it is God himself who makes the plea through us, his fellow workers (1 Cor. 3:9; 2 Cor. 5:20; 6:1), and his Spirit who guarantees that his Word will not return void (Isa. 55:11). We are to plant and water faithfully, confidently trusting that God will give the increase (1 Cor. 3:7).

So biblical evangelism requires of us one thing primarily: that we be faithful to share the good news of Jesus Christ with the people God places in contact with us (1 Cor. 4:1–2). Specifically, faithful evangelism must (1) be content specific, presenting the truth about "who God is, who men are, what sin is, who Jesus is, what Jesus has done about sin, and what we must do about what Jesus has done;" (2) "include the notion that Christ is the exclusive way of salvation," barring the idea that there are multiple paths leading to God (John 14:6; Acts 4:12); and (3) call the hearer to repentance and faith in Christ.[2]

Biblical evangelism requires sharing the wonderful news that Christ died for sinners and then calling our hearers to repent and believe. John the Baptist preached this message (Matt. 3:1–2). Jesus proclaimed this same gospel (Matt. 4:17). And the apostle Peter at Pentecost heralded this same good news (Acts 2:38). The healthy church member makes this message central as he or she seeks to be a faithful biblical evangelist.

Doing the Work of an Evangelist

Several writers have written to help us with the work of faithfully proclaiming the good news of Jesus Christ. Some have given very helpful and practical suggestions. Mark Dever outlines six things church members should keep in mind in evangelism.[3]

1) Tell people with honesty that if they repent and believe they will be saved—but it will be costly.
2) Tell people with urgency that if they repent and believe they will be saved—but they must decide now.
3) Tell people with joy that if they repent and believe the good news they will be saved. However difficult it may be, it is all worth it!
4) Use the Bible.

5) Realize that the lives of the individual Christian and of the church as a whole are a central part of evangelism. Both should give credibility to the gospel we proclaim.

6) Remember to pray.

Michael P. Andrus offers some additional helpful advice. In order to keep a healthy view of conversion in mind in our evangelistic efforts, he suggests:

1) Counsel seekers in a way that focuses on deeds, not words; a change of life, not just a change of beliefs. The last thing we should communicate is that by merely saying yes to a proposition, they can be assured of eternal life.

2) Focus on a biblical, serious view of sin and guilt.

3) Teach the Bible and Christian doctrine so that potential converts grasp that the plan of salvation is God's counsel, not human wisdom.

4) Abandon the facile language of *decisionism* ("just believe," "pray to receive," "invite Jesus into your heart") in favor of the more rigorous language of conversion ("surrender to the Lordship of Jesus Christ" or "turn from sin, accept the forgiveness purchased by Jesus through his death, and live a life of obedience to him").[4]

The Local Church in Evangelism

In addition to these excellent recommendations, a church member should recognize the centrality and usefulness of the local church in evangelism. Where we are involved in gospel-preaching churches, then by God's grace the gospel will be preached in each Lord's Day gathering. Inviting our non-Christian friends to church services is an excellent way to expand on the personal conversations you have had with them about the gospel.

It's also an opportunity for them to see the gospel "fleshed out" in the lives of an actual congregation of believers. In the church, non-Christians should see the kind of unity and love that testifies to the truth and power of the gospel and God's love (John 13:34–35; 17:20–21). Our friends will see the gospel with their eyes as they witness Christians observing baptism and the Lord's Supper. Both in the way we live together as a church and in the ordinances of the church, we display the gospel in ways that complement the preached word of the gospel.

Moreover, involving our non-Christian family and friends in our church life is a helpful preview of the life they will be called to live should the Lord bring them to repentance and saving faith. Making the local church a central part of our evangelistic efforts helps to cut the root of spiritual individualism at the beginning of the Christian life.

Finally, in our local churches we have at our disposal perhaps dozens or hundreds of allies—fellow Christians—each with their own conversion experiences and resources, who can build relationships with our friends and families. The Lord is often pleased to use our fellow members in sharing the pivotal word or living the compelling example that brings another person to saving faith. Don't leave the local church out of your efforts to win the lost!

Conclusion

I once attended an evangelism conference sponsored by a local church. The main speaker for the conference asked the audience what they thought was the number-one reason for Christians not doing the work of an evangelist. The audience gave a number of good answers, ranging from fear, lack of knowledge, and indifference. The speaker stunned the audience when he suggested that those are certainly problems, but that the number-one problem is that too many Christians do not believe Romans 1:16. They do not believe the gospel is the power of God for salvation. They lack confidence in the gospel.

How about you? Are you confident that the gospel is the power of God to save? Does your work as an evangelist demonstrate such confidence? I pray that we all can answer "yes" to these questions.

For Further Reflection

1. Does the way you speak to others about Jesus include all the essential ideas of the gospel?

2. Does the way you speak to others about Jesus demonstrate confidence in the gospel message itself, that it is the power of God for salvation?

3. How would a church with members deeply committed to each other change the perception of the church in the community?

For Further Reading

Carson, D. A., ed. *Telling the Truth: Evangelizing Postmoderns.* Grand Rapids, MI: Zondervan, 2000.

Dever, Mark E. *The Gospel and Personal Evangelism.* Wheaton, IL: Crossway, 2007.

Metzger, Will. *Tell the Truth: The Whole Gospel to the Whole Person by Whole People.* Downers Grove, IL: InterVarsity, 2002.

Packer, J. I. *Evangelism and the Sovereignty of God.* Downers Grove, IL: InterVarsity, 1991.

Stiles, Mack. *Speaking of Jesus: How to Tell Your Friends the Best News They Will Ever Hear.* Downers Grove, IL: InterVarsity, 1995.

A HEALTHY CHURCH MEMBER IS A COMMITTED MEMBER

As a young man, Joshua Harris's attitude toward the church reflected that of many people today. Harris writes:

> When I graduated from my church's high school youth group, I started visiting around. I loved God and had big dreams for how I wanted to serve Him, but I didn't see any reason to get too involved in one church. By then, I thought I knew all there was to know about church, and I wasn't impressed. Most churches struck me as out-of-date and out-of-touch. There had to be better, more efficient ways to accomplish great things for God.[1]

He considered the church secondary, outmoded, inefficient, and a hindrance. It wasn't that he didn't love God or God's people. He just didn't think that belonging to a particular church was important, and might even be a hindrance.

Joshua is not alone. Many people think that church—especially church membership, that is, actually signing up and joining—is a spiritual relic destined to hinder spiritual freedom and fruitfulness.

The reasons for this view of church membership are many. Some Christians are just plain *indifferent* to church membership. They can take it or leave it; they're neither excited nor negative toward the church. It just doesn't matter to them.

Others are *ignorant*. They are uninformed. They've never considered the Bible's view of the local church.

Still others are *indecisive*. They can't make up their minds about joining. Perhaps they're the kind of people who never really make decisions; decisions tend to happen to them.

And there are the *independent* types. They are "Lone Ranger Christians" who don't want to be saddled with the burdens of church membership. They don't want people "in their business." They want to come into a church, consume what they need, and leave unattached.

Finally, there are those who are slow to commit to a local church because their affections are *inverted*. They have strong attachments to a "home church" in the town they grew up in, and yet their bodies are hundreds of miles away. They can't bring themselves to join a church where they live because they've never emotionally left a church from their past.

At root, all of these perspectives on the local church stem from the same problem: a failure to understand or take seriously God's intent that the local church be central to the life of his people. People don't become committed church members—and therefore healthy Christians—because they don't understand that such a commitment is precisely how God intends his people to live out the faith and experience Christian love.

Is "Church Membership" a Biblical Idea?

When people who encounter for the first time the idea that church membership is necessary and important, many want to know, "Is the idea of church membership important? Where can I find it in the Bible?"

As with so many things, you can't turn in the Bible to "the Book of Church Membership" or to a chapter conveniently labeled by Bible publishers, "On Becoming a Member." The biblical data isn't as obvious as that, yet the idea of membership is nearly everywhere in Scripture.

Have you ever considered how many practices and commands given to the New Testament church lose all their meaning if membership is not practiced, visibly identifiable, and important? Here are a few essential things commanded in Scripture for the local church that would lose their meaning without an operational concept of membership.[2]

CHURCH LEADERSHIP

Two classic passages in Scripture outline for the church the qualifications its leaders must have (1 Tim. 3:1–13; Titus 1:5–9). In addition to these qualifications, there are explicit commands for leaders to shepherd the flock and for Christians to submit to their leaders (Heb. 13:17). Yet if there is no identifiable membership, there is no one for leaders to lead. Submission to their authority as Hebrews 13:17 requires becomes nonsense if the leaders are not responsible for a group, and that group is not attached to them in some way.

CHURCH DISCIPLINE

In 1 Corinthians 5, the apostle Paul instructs the believers in Corinth to "put out of their fellowship" a man involved in sexual immorality. The Lord Jesus commanded a similar action in Matthew 18:15–17. Part of the reason the Bible commands the practice of church discipline is so that clear distinctions can be maintained between God's people, the church, and the surrounding world (1 Cor. 5:9–13). If there is no practical, visible way of determining who belongs to the church and who belongs to the world, this distinction is lost, and "putting out of fellowship" is an impossible feat since there is no real way of being in the fellowship.

KEEPING LISTS AND VOTING

There is slight evidence that the early church kept some lists associated with its membership. For example, lists of widows were kept (1 Tim. 5:9). Also, Christians in the local church voted for some actions. It was the "majority" who voted to remove the man from membership in the church at Corinth (2 Cor. 2:6).

Electing leaders, submitting to them, regulating membership, keeping lists, and voting only make sense if a known, identifiable, and distinct body is recognized. So while the Bible doesn't provide us with a biblical treatise on membership per se, there is enough evidence in the inspired record to suggest that some form of membership was practiced and was necessary to the church's operation. Church membership is no less important in our day.

The Essence of Membership: Committed Love

Our Lord Jesus specified one defining mark for his disciples. Of course, there are many marks of true discipleship, but one mark is singled out as signifying to the watching world that we belong to Christ:

> A new commandment I give you, that you love one another: just as I have loved you, you also are to love one another. By this all people will know that you are my disciples, if you have love for one another. (John 13:34–35)

The mark of Christian discipleship is love—love of the kind that Jesus exercised toward his followers, love visible enough that men will recognize it as belonging to those people who follow Jesus.

Not surprisingly, then, a healthy Christian is one who is committed to expressing this kind of love toward other Christians. And the best place for Christians to love this way is in the assembly of God's people called the local church. Is it no wonder then that the author of Hebrews instructs us to "consider how to stir up one another to love and good works," and then right away says "not neglecting to meet together, as is the habit of some, but encouraging one another, and all the more as you see the Day drawing near" (Heb. 10:24–25)? Faithful church attendance is associated tightly with stirring each other to love and good deeds. The local church is the place where love is most visibly and compellingly displayed among God's people. It's where the "body of Christ" is most plainly represented in the world.

What Does a Committed Church Member Look Like?

In one sense the question "What does a committed church member look like?" is what this entire book is about. But here we want to explore this question in relation to the essential command and mark of love. Below are ways committed membership expresses itself.

ATTENDS REGULARLY

This is the first and most important ministry of every Christian in the local church. Being present, being known, and being active are the only ways to make Christian love possible (Heb. 10:24–25).

SEEKS PEACE

A committed church member is committed to the maintenance of peace in the congregation. "Let us pursue what makes for peace and mutual upbuilding" (Rom. 14:19). "And a harvest of righteousness is sown in peace by those who make peace" (James 3:18).

EDIFIES OTHERS

The one consistent purpose or goal of the public meeting of the church is mutual edification, building each other up in the faith (1 Cor. 12, 14; Eph. 4:11–16). A healthy and committed member comes to serve, not to be served, like Jesus (Mark 10:45); to provide, not to be a consumer only.

WARNS AND ADMONISHES OTHERS

This is discussed at greater length in chapter 6, "Seeks Discipline." A committed member is committed to speaking the truth in love to his brothers and sisters, to helping them avoid pitfalls, and to encouraging them in holiness and Christian joy. A committed member will not be wrongly intrusive in the lives of others—a busybody—but he also will not be "hands off" when it comes to caring for and counseling others.

PURSUES RECONCILIATION

Christians are people who are reconciled to God through Christ. As a consequence, we have been given "the ministry of reconciliation" (2 Cor. 5:18–21). So, a committed member strives to repair breaches as quickly as possible, even before continuing in public worship (Matt. 5:23–24).

BEARS WITH OTHERS

Ministers of reconciliation must be patient and longsuffering. They must be characterized by meekness such that they do not think more highly of themselves than they ought (Matt. 5:5). They must hold up under the weight of disappointments, frustrations, loss, attack, slander, and offense (Matt. 18:21–22; Rom. 15:1). By carrying each others' burdens we fulfill the law of Christ (Gal. 6:2).

PREPARES FOR THE ORDINANCES

One privilege of church membership is participating in Christ's ordinances—baptism and communion. Moreover, these privileges give us visible proclamations of the good news that Christ died for sinners and rose again to eternal life. So it's a great tragedy that many Christians neglect the ordinances that Jesus himself established 2,000 years ago. A committed member rejoices at the baptism of new believers, and he examines his heart in preparation for joining the family of God at the

Lord's Table. He receives these spiritual exercises as means of grace, means that give visible testimony to the effect of the gospel in his life and the life of the gathered church.

SUPPORTS THE WORK OF THE MINISTRY

A committed member gives resources, time, and talent to the furtherance of the gospel in the local church. He lives out the Bible's call to the body of Christ. "We have different gifts, according to the grace given us. If a man's gift is prophesying, let him use it in proportion to his faith. If it is serving, let him serve; if it is teaching, let him teach; if it is encouraging, let him encourage; if it is contributing to the needs of others, let him give generously; if it is leadership, let him govern diligently; if it is showing mercy, let him do it cheerfully" (Rom. 12:6–8). A healthy, committed church member receives and applies the grace of God by working to support the ministry of the local church and excels in giving what he has already received from God to gospel work. He should follow the example of the Macedonians, who committed to a financial giving strategy that was sacrificial, generous, increasing over time, and fueled by faith in God despite present circumstances (2 Cor. 8–9). What do we have that we did not first receive from God? What do we have that we should not be willing to give back to him in worship?

Conclusion

To fail to associate ourselves in a lasting and committed way with the Head of the church by joining his body is surely a sign of ingratitude, whether from an uninformed or a dull heart. We who have the privilege of living in countries where we may freely join a local church should keep this admonition from Dietrich Bonhoeffer in mind:

> It is by the grace of God that a congregation is permitted to gather visibly in this world to share God's Word and sacrament. Not all Christians receive this blessing. The imprisoned, the sick, the scattered lonely, the proclaimers of the Gospel in heathen lands stand alone. They know that visible fellowship is a blessing. They remember, as the Psalmist did, how they went "with the multitude . . . to the house of God, with the voice of joy and praise, with a multitude that kept holyday (Ps. 42:4). . . . Therefore, let him who until now has had the privilege of living in common Christian life with other Christians praise God's grace from the bottom of his heart. Let him thank God on his knees and declare: It is grace, nothing but grace, that we are allowed to live in community with Christian brethren.[3]

For Further Reflection

1. On a scale of 1 to 10, how would you rate your commitment to membership in your local church? If your rating is not a 10, why?

2. In general, does your local church give appropriate attention to church membership? Can you cite particular passages of Scripture to support your answer?

3. How would a church with members deeply committed to each other change the perception of the church in the community?

For Further Reading

Bonhoeffer, Dietrich. *Life Together*. New York: Harper and Row, 1954.

Harris, Joshua. *Stop Dating the Church*. Sisters, OR: Multnomah, 2004.

A HEALTHY CHURCH MEMBER SEEKS DISCIPLINE

Life needs to be ordered. That's a simple truth too often forgotten or overlooked. In order to thrive and grow, all life needs order.

Chaos, then, is the enemy of growth. Disorganization, sloppiness, and inattention generally introduce the kind of instability that weakens rather than strengthens. Where there is no order there will likely be little in the environment that sustains and nourishes. Life needs to be ordered.

Young married couples discover this when God gives them children. Their lives up to this point may have been characterized by a "foot loose and fancy free" attitude, but they soon realize that in order to properly care for and raise a child they will need to maintain a certain amount of order. Sleep and feeding routines must be established. Small and dangerous objects must be removed. Outlets must be covered. Diaper changes, baths, fresh clothing all must be provided at the right times. Order must reign if growth is to occur. It's a fact of life.

Well, order is also necessary in spiritual matters. Without

the proper establishment of routines, boundaries, and patterns, thriving spiritually most likely will not occur or will be haphazard at best. Another word for the order needed to grow spiritually is *discipline*.

What Is Discipline?

Today, when people hear the word *discipline*, they most likely think of negative forms of punishment, like spanking a rebellious child. To many, discipline sounds harsh, something to be avoided or something that only unkind or unmerciful people pursue. For others, it sounds restrictive of freedom and joy. To be sure, discipline is not always a pleasant experience. The writer in Hebrews makes this point: "For the moment all discipline seems painful rather than pleasant" (Heb. 12:11).

But actually, the word *discipline* has a much broader and more positive meaning than "unpleasant punishment." *Discipline* and *disciple* share the same Latin root and are tied closely to the idea of education and order. The disciple is a student, one who participates in a certain discipline, who learns a profession, or who masters a body of thought. Such a person has his or her life ordered under or by the rules of a trade. So, professional athletes abide by the rules of their sports. Psychology professors dedicate themselves to this or that school of thought. Doctors adhere to the principles of the American Medical Association or the Hippocratic Oath. All of these are disciples of and disciplined by the principles of their field.

The same is true with the church. The church is a place where everything in the gathered services should "be done decently and in order" (1 Cor. 14:40). That order is necessary for edification.

And discipline is necessary in the lives of individual believers as well.[1] Jay Adams summarized the connection between orderly discipline, learning, and the Christian life well: "When we are baptized into the church, we thereby matriculate into Christ's school. Then, for the rest of our earthly life, we are to be taught (not facts alone, but also) to obey the commands of Christ. This is education with force, education backed up by the discipline of good order that is necessary for learning to take place."[2]

So discipline is about education and learning, order and growth. It is discipline in the life of the congregation and the healthy church member that provides an atmosphere for growth and development. It leads to the rare polished jewel of Christlikeness.

What Does Discipline Look Like in the Life of a Healthy Church Member?

Two forms of discipline occur in the life of healthy congregations and church members. Both of these approaches to discipline have their origin in the Word of God, and, in fact, are two ways of understanding the purpose and effect of God's Word in the life of his people.

The apostle writes in 2 Timothy 3:16, "All Scripture is breathed out by God and profitable for teaching, for reproof, for correction, and for training in righteousness."

In other words, the Scripture, which is "breathed out" or inspired by God, has two general purposes: *formative discipline* and *corrective discipline*. When Paul writes that the Scripture is "profitable for teaching" and "for training in righteousness," he is describing positive or formative discipline.

Formative discipline refers to how Scripture shapes and molds the Christian as he or she imbibes its teaching and is trained to live for God. While medical doctors are governed by the standards and oaths of their profession, Christians are shaped and governed by the Word of God.

Likewise, when Paul refers to the Scriptures as profitable "for reproof, for correction" he is describing how the Word of God confronts us and turns us away from error to righteousness. This is corrective discipline.

The vast majority of discipline in any church will be positive or formative discipline as people grow from the preached Word, as they study the Scriptures in personal devotion, and as they are shaped by fellowship and encouragement from brethren in Christ. But from time to time a brother or sister will indulge in sin and need loving reproof or correction from other members of the church who are committed to the welfare of his or her soul. Moreover, the Scriptures address various situations requiring correction. Our Lord Jesus outlined a process for corrective discipline in cases where one brother sins against another (Matt. 18:15–17). The apostle Paul exhorted the Corinthian church to confront and expel from membership a brother taken in scandalous sexual sin (1 Corinthians 5). And not only is the church's correction necessary for the "really bad" sins like sexual immorality, but even the seemingly more mundane, disorderly sins such as laziness and false teaching warrant correction (2 Thess. 3:6, 11; Titus 3:10).

No one lives an entire life without the need of discipline, whether positive or corrective. So the healthy church member embraces discipline as one means of grace in the Christian life.

How Do We Joyfully Seek Discipline?

The topic of church discipline may be new to you. Or maybe the topic isn't new, but the practice of discipline in your local church may be quite new or nonexistent. Some people will have to simultaneously grow in their understanding of this important topic, confront fears or wrong impressions, and contribute to their church's health. What follows are a few suggestions for cultivating a desire for both positive and corrective discipline so that we might be healthy members of our churches.

RECEIVE THE WORD OF GOD WITH MEEKNESS

James calls Christians to "put away all filthiness and rampant wickedness and receive with meekness the implanted word, which is able to save your souls" (James 1:21). Implicit in James's instruction is a distinction between an ungodly life of filthiness and wickedness and the Christlike life of humility or meekness. Christians should receive the Word of God with meekness. That is, in the preaching of God's Word and in Bible study, Christians should remain lowly and gentle before the Scripture, acknowledging it as the source of salvation and instruction in godly living. As we come to the Scripture, we are to do so as people knowing our sinful nature, our spiritual poverty before God, and our need for the molding influence of God, which comes normally by his Word.

How can we know if we are receiving God's Word with meekness? Perhaps the following questions will help:

- As we read the Bible, are we reading for information only or with faith that God actually speaks through his Word?

- When we hear the Word preached, are we generally looking to have a need met (for example, to be entertained or to gather some practical advice) or are we primarily desiring to understand the original meaning of the text and apply it to our lives?
- Is our first reaction to the Scripture "how does this make me feel?" or "do I accept this as true?" Do we allow our feelings to determine what's true, or do we allow the Scriptures to determine our feelings?[3]
- Is our listening posture during sermons or Scripture readings defensive or combative, as though we demand someone to "prove it to us"?[4]
- Do we tend to judge other philosophies and viewpoints by the Scripture, or do we try to either reconcile or judge the Scripture by other philosophies and views?

Receiving the Word with meekness means accepting the Bible by faith, with a friendly and submissive heart, and with the testimony of God's Spirit. Specifically, we accept the fact that the Bible is true, that it's the only sufficient authority for shaping our lives, and that it must govern how we feel and think. By doing so, the healthy church member prepares himself for the formative discipline of Christ's church.

LEARN TO RECOGNIZE CHASTISEMENT AS EVIDENCE OF GOD'S LOVE

If you are troubled by the perception that church discipline is unkind or unloving, consider the fact that the Bible tells us that God himself is a loving Father who disciplines his children: "My son, do not regard lightly the discipline of the Lord, nor be weary when reproved by him. For the Lord disciplines the one he loves, and chastises every son whom he receives" (Heb. 12:5–6).

Receiving discipline at the hand of God is evidence of his love for us. Wherever he reproves and chastises us, we can be certain that he is treating us as a father would treat a son. Discipline is an act of love, not of vengeance or hatred. The writer in Hebrews goes on to state, "It is for discipline that you have to endure. God is treating you as sons. For what son is there whom his father does not discipline?" (Heb. 12:7).

And what is the goal of this loving Father's discipline? He does it that we might "be subject to the Father of spirits and live" and "share his holiness" (Heb. 12:9–10). In love, the Father is protecting our lives and conforming us to his holiness as he corrects and chastises us. A healthy church member recognizes this chastisement as love and accepts it as one source of assurance, since those who are not so chastised are "illegitimate children and not sons" (Heb. 12:8).

HUMBLY ACCEPT CORRECTION FROM OTHERS

Not only do healthy church members accept the Lord's chastisement, but they humbly accept correction from others. They recognize that often the Lord's correction comes through other members in the church, saints who care enough not only to encourage in good times but to confront and correct when necessary. Healthy church members agree that "better is open rebuke than hidden love. Faithful are the wounds of a friend" (Prov. 27:5–6).

Many churches that take membership seriously ask new members to review, support, and sometimes sign their church's covenant. A church covenant is a document that briefly summarizes the commitment church members make before the Lord and to each other to live out the Christian faith in a manner ordered by Scripture.

One of my favorite lines in a typical church covenant addresses this important issue of accepting love and correction from others:

> We will walk together in brotherly love, as becomes the members of a Christian Church, exercise an affectionate care and watchfulness over each other and faithfully admonish and entreat one another as occasion may require.[5]

"Fools despise wisdom and instruction" (Prov. 1:7), but it is the nature of true godliness, maturity, and health in church members to accept the loving instruction and rebuke of others.

TAKE SERIOUSLY OUR RESPONSIBILITY TO DISCIPLINE OTHERS

A fourth way we may cultivate a healthy desire for godly discipline is to take seriously our responsibility to care for others in this way. Here's another line in a typical church covenant that addresses this responsibility: "We will work together for the continuance of a faithful evangelical ministry in this church, as we sustain its worship, ordinances, discipline, and doctrines." It is a basic responsibility and privilege of every church member to help sustain the discipline of the local church. This is why the classic passages, such as Matthew 18 and 1 Corinthians 5, dealing with unrepentant sin conclude with a final and decisive action by the congregation.[6] But not only does correction belong to the congregation as a whole;

it begins as each individual is proactive in love and seeks to restore those who are caught in sin.[7]

DON'T FORGET TO REJOICE!

It may be easy to think of church discipline only in terms of the grief and sorrow that accompany sin and the loss of a brother or sister. And such grief has its place (Matt. 5:4; 1 Cor. 5:2). But the entire process of discipline, from the formative work of the Word to the corrective work of the church in sometimes removing an unrepentant member, should be undertaken with hope and the goal of repentance that leads to rejoicing and comfort (2 Cor. 2:6). We are endeavoring to win our brothers and sisters to the truth (James 5:19–20), and when that happens we are to rejoice along with the courts of heaven. Perhaps nothing is quite as sweet as seeing a person who is deceived and being destroyed by sin break free from sin's merciless grip and discover afresh the freedom and forgiveness of our merciful Savior. As healthy church members endeavoring to strengthen our churches, we can participate in the discipline of the church with joy and faith, knowing that our loving Father graciously and faithfully corrects those whom he loves. It's our delight to see the tracings of God's handiwork displayed in the growth, repentance, and restoration of those who receive the grace of discipline.

Conclusion

It is impossible for members of a church to care effectively for each other if only a few people own the responsibility of correcting or instructing brothers or sisters in need of it. If members don't give themselves to serving others by teaching the

Word in Sunday school or leading small groups, if members shy away from getting to know one another so that there is no context for meaningful fellowship, then neither positive nor corrective discipline will occur. The house of God will be inadequately ordered, his children poorly taught, and the witness of the church tarnished by unrepentant and uncorrected sin.

For Further Reflection

With a group of Christian friends and church members, consider and discuss the questions listed on pages 77–78.

For Further Reading

Adams, Jay. *Handbook on Church Discipline: A Right and Privilege of Every Church Member*. Grand Rapids, MI: Zondervan, 1974.

Lauterbach, Mark. *The Transforming Community: The Practice of the Gospel in Church Discipline*. Ross-shire, Christian Focus, 2003.

For Pastors

Dagg, John L. *Manual of Church Order*. Harrisonburg, VA: Gano Books, 1990; first published 1858.

Dever, Mark E., ed. *Polity: Biblical Arguments on How to Conduct Church Life*. Washington, DC: 9Marks Ministries, 2001.

Wills, Gregory. *Democratic Religion: Freedom, Authority, and Church Discipline in the Baptist South, 1785–1900*. Oxford University Press, 2003.

Wray, Daniel. *Biblical Church Discipline*. Edinburgh: Banner of Truth, 1978.

A HEALTHY CHURCH MEMBER IS A GROWING DISCIPLE

A healthy church member is a growing church member.

It is impossible to separate the health of a local church from the health of its members. And it's impossible to divide the well-being of a church member from his or her spiritual growth and discipleship.

When Christians Do Not Grow

This is speculation on my part, but it may be the case that the most chronic problem facing churches and Christians is the lack of consistent spiritual growth and progress in discipleship. We all know Christians who have confessed faith and repentance, yet who sadly admit that they have not grown in some time. This situation comes in two varieties. There is the temporary plateau or spiritual rut that every Christian experiences and must overcome from time to time. This is normal and shouldn't cause too much alarm. Perhaps routines need to be changed or focus renewed, but the problem isn't chronic yet.

But then there is the chronic variety. Here, people may not

be able to perceive much growth over a prolonged period of time. They've fallen into something deeper than a rut. They're not just "stuck," struggling to get free; they've settled into a spiritual slumber. If they have been in this sleep for some time, perhaps they believe that there is no more growth to be had or even that following Christ is a shallow, hollow thing. The expectation of growth may be abandoned. Pride may be asserting, "I've arrived spiritually and there's really not much more growing to do."

Where this happens there should be great alarm! In our largely individualistic and privatized spiritual worlds, such trouble can go unnoticed, unspoken, and uncorrected for some time.

Advancement in the knowledge and likeness of Christ, spiritual maturity and progress toward it, are supposed to be normal for the Christian. So Hebrews exhorts us to "leave the elementary doctrine of Christ and go on to maturity" (Heb. 6:1). The writer assumes that these Christians should have progressed "by this time . . . to be teachers," having moved from "milk" for the unskilled child to "solid food . . . for the mature" (Heb. 5:11–13).

Speaking of himself, the apostle Paul modeled how to maintain humility when it comes to spiritual growth:

Not that I have already obtained this or am already perfect, but I press on to make it my own, because Christ Jesus has made me his own. Brothers, I do not consider that I have made it on my own. But one thing I do: forgetting what lies behind and straining forward to what lies ahead, I press on toward the goal for the prize of the upward call of God in Christ Jesus. (Phil. 3:12–14)

Then he gives this exhortation to his readers, "Let those of us who are mature think this way" (v. 15a).

It is normal for Christians to grow, to work for growth, and to expect increasing spiritual maturity. Those who do are healthy church members.

Problems in Our Thinking about Growth

But saying that a Christian should expect, work for, and experience growth isn't the end of the issue. For the Christian to grow in a healthy way, we must clarify what growth is and is not. Ours is a superficial culture that lays emphasis on the outward signs and neglects the inward reality. We're far too vulnerable to settling for being thought of as mature rather than actually being mature.

Jesus' teaching in Luke 18 helps us to identify at least two attitudes that hinder solid biblical growth and discipleship:

> He . . . told this parable to some who trusted in themselves that they were righteous, and treated others with contempt: "Two men went up into the temple to pray, one a Pharisee and the other a tax collector. The Pharisee, standing by himself, prayed thus: 'God, I thank you that I am not like other men, extortioners, unjust, adulterers, or even like this tax collector. I fast twice a week; I give tithes of all that I get.' But the tax collector, standing far off, would not even lift up his eyes to heaven, but beat his breast, saying, 'God, be merciful to me, a sinner!' I tell you, this man went down to his house justified, rather than the other. For everyone who exalts himself will be humbled, but the one who humbles himself will be exalted." (Luke 18:9–14)

Three problems in the Pharisee's thinking prevented him from growing in godliness.

1) *The performance trap.* In all major sports, statistics are recorded for player performance—batting percentage, field goal percentage, number of stolen bases, home runs, touchdowns, assists, and on and on. Often the worth of an athlete is summed up by these statistics. And those who can "stuff the stat sheet" with big numbers are celebrated, heralded as "marquis players," and given awards.

Our idea of Christian growth can be influenced by a "stuffing the stat sheet" mindset. Notice the Pharisee spoke with God about himself and all he had done. He measured growth in observable goals and objectives—fasting twice a week and giving tithes of all he received. We can do this too. We emphasize the number of times we completed "quiet times" this week, the number of times we passed Christian literature to others, or how often we shared the gospel. We can fall into the performance trap, thinking that spiritual growth and discipleship look like good performance and success. When this happens our sense of growth and worth become wrongly tied up with our "stats."

2) *Judging by the wrong standards.* Another thing that often misguides Christians when it comes to growth is the tendency to judge our well-being by comparing ourselves to others. Many Christians are relativists in this way. The Pharisee was proud before God that he "was not like other men, extortioners, unjust, adulterers, or even like this tax collector." Imagine that! Kneeling to pray before God and simultaneously judging and denouncing the man praying right

next to him! Jonathan Edwards's eighth resolution is a better approach. Edwards wrote:

> Resolved, To act, in all respects, both speaking and doing, as if nobody had been so vile as I, and as if I had committed the same sins, or had the same infirmities or failings, as others, and that I will let the knowledge of their failings promote nothing but shame in myself, and prove only an occasion of my confessing my own sins and misery to God.[1]

If we're focusing on others in an attempt to justify ourselves before God or to "exalt ourselves" as "giants of the faith," we will not only *not* grow as we ought, but we will also delude ourselves into thinking we're better than we are. And we may be sure that God will humble us. So it is better to humble ourselves and trust in the grace of God than to be opposed by God because of pride (James 4:6; 1 Pet. 5:5).

3) Depending on personal strength or effort in spiritual growth. This is another of the Pharisee's mistakes. As far as he is concerned, all that should commend him before God is a result of his effort and ability. But self-effort is not the source of true spiritual growth. After the writer to the Hebrews exhorts them to "leave the elementary doctrines of Christ and go on to maturity," he adds, "And this we will do if God permits" (Heb. 6:1, 3). Holy Scripture tells us that our progress in discipleship and spiritual maturity depends on the grace and will of God, not on our self-effort and strength. This is why the apostle Paul praises God for the growth of Christians (2 Thess. 1:3) and prays to God for continued growth (1 Thess. 3:11–13; Col. 1:10). We are commanded to grow and to cultivate maturity and godliness (2 Pet. 1:5–8, 3:18, for example), but all of our efforts are exercised in dependence upon God and with faith in him for the growth we seek.

So biblical growth should not be confused with outward performance alone, nor is it measured by using others as our standard. And it does not finally depend on our self-effort and attainments. What, then, is growth and how does the healthy church member pursue it?

The Growth We Want to See

A healthy church member has a pervasive concern for his or her own personal growth and the growth of other members of her or his church. As Mark Dever correctly notes, "Working to promote Christian discipleship and growth is working to bring glory not to ourselves but to God. This is how God will make himself known in the world."[2] Since a concern for God's glory should be uppermost in our lives as believers, our concern for growth should be pervasive.

Several passages of Scripture outline for us the kind of growth healthy church members should hope to see in themselves and others. For example, Galatians 5:22–25 lists for us the fruit of the Spirit, evidences of Spirit-wrought virtue and character that typify those who live not according to their own power and sinful nature but by the Spirit. We are to "grow in the grace and knowledge of our Lord and Savior Jesus Christ" (2 Pet. 3:18).

Ephesians 4:11–13 reminds us that the Lord gives gifted men to the church for the purpose of growth "for building up the body of Christ, until we all attain to the unity of the faith and of the knowledge of the Son of God, to mature manhood, to the measure of the stature of the fullness of Christ."

We can sum up all of these pictures and exhortations with either the term "godliness" or "holiness." The growth we wish to see, the growth that is not finally external and superficial, is growth in godliness or holiness, growth in "the stature of the fullness of Christ." A growing church member is someone who looks more and more like Jesus in attitude of heart, thought, speech, and action. That's what we long to be and long for our churches to be.

Growing to Be Like Jesus

How do healthy church members cultivate such growth? The following are some suggestions for continuing to develop godliness or holiness in life.

ABIDE IN CHRIST

Jesus said:

> "I am the vine; you are the branches. If a man remains in me and I in him, he will bear much fruit; apart from me you can do nothing. If anyone does not remain in me, he is like a branch that is thrown away and withers; such branches are picked up, thrown into the fire and burned. If you remain in me and my words remain in you, ask whatever you wish, and it will be given you. This is to my Father's glory, that you bear much fruit, showing yourselves to be my disciples." (John 15:5–8)

The key to growth in godliness is remaining in the True Vine, who is Christ Jesus. Here, remaining in Christ and bearing fruit is "nothing less than the outcome of persevering dependence on the vine, driven by faith, embracing all of the believer's life and the product of his witness."[3] And this fruitfulness comes as the Word of the Lord remains in the disciple. "Such words must so lodge in the disciple's mind and heart that conformity to Christ, obedience to Christ, is the most natural (supernatural?) thing in the world."[4] Abiding in Christ, remaining in his Word, is essential to proper Christian discipleship and growth.

USE THE ORDINARY MEANS OF GRACE

Many Christians seem to believe advancement in spiritual maturity must come through some extraordinary or "breakthrough" experience. For them, it's the fantastic that produces growth. But as we've just seen in John 15, it is the ordinary means of grace that ordinarily produces growth and maturity. In fact, while the sensational and extraordinary can and often does lead people astray, the Word properly taught and understood never will. The "ordinary means of grace" include the study of the Word of God, participation in the ordinances of baptism and communion along with the gathered church, and prayer. These are the customary ways in which the grace of God is proclaimed, displayed, and appropriated in the Christian life. By the Word of God, we hear Christ revealed and glorified, and there we "learn Christ" most clearly. But in the ordinances of baptism and communion, we see Christ and the gospel as we picture his death, burial, and resurrection for us and for our salvation.

A healthy Christian does not neglect these ordinances and means of grace but rejoices in them, prepares for them, and is reminded through the senses of the glories of Christ our

Savior. She or he remembers that grace "teaches [or trains] us to renounce ungodliness and worldly passions, and to live self-controlled, upright, and godly lives in the present age" (Titus 2:11–12). A healthy Christian relies more and more on the grace of God as it is communicated through the Word and the ordinances.

PARTICIPATE IN THE LOCAL CHURCH

Hebrews 10:25 instructs us not to neglect the assembly of the saints. Instead, we are to gather and encourage one another more and more as we await Jesus' return. The public assembly is meant for the edification, the building up, the growth of the Christian. Neglecting to participate in the corporate life of the church or failing to actively serve and be served is a sure-fire way to limit our growth. Ephesians 4:11–16 offers a pretty strong argument that participation in the body of Christ is the main way in which Christ strengthens and matures us. When we serve others in the church, bear with one another, love one another, correct one another, and encourage one another, we participate in a kind of "spiritual maturity co-op" where our stores and supplies are multiplied. The end result is growth and discipleship.

LOOK TO JESUS' COMING

Finally, we grow in holiness by meditating on and looking forward to the coming of Jesus. Most of the New Testament references to Jesus' return are connected with some exhortation to holiness and purity. For example, in Matthew 25 when Jesus finishes teaching the disciples about his second coming, he concludes with the simple exhortation to "be ready," to look for his return, and to live a fitting life in the meantime. Matthew 26 follows with three parables, all exhorting his hearers to watch and to be faithful until he returns. The Lord taught that his second coming is something for us to meditate upon consistently, and that that meditation should lead us to guard our lives and to grow.

Titus 2:13–14 refers to the "blessed hope, the appearing of the glory of our great God and Savior Jesus Christ" with this explanation of Jesus' mission: "[He] gave himself for us to redeem us from all lawlessness and to purify for himself a people for his own possession who are zealous for good works." In other words, we look to the cross and the second coming of Christ and remember that Christ has done every-thing for our redemption, purity, and zeal—our holiness. The apostle John includes a very similar statement in one of his letters. He writes:

> Beloved, we are God's children now, and what we will be has not yet appeared; but we know that when he appears we shall be like him, because we shall see him as he is. And everyone who thus hopes in him purifies himself as he is pure. (1 John 3:2–3)

Our yearning to be *with* Jesus and to *see* Jesus is intended to make us more *like* Jesus in holiness. Looking forward to Christ will produce growth in healthy church members.

Conclusion

The healthy church member is a growing church member. Specifically, she or he is a church member that grows in Christlikeness, holiness, and maturity. That maturity and holi-ness are developed in dependence upon Christ, his Word, and others in the local church. And most wonderful of all, we will not stop growing until we reach the fullness of Christ!

For Further Reflection

1. Are there any wrong ways you have been measuring or thinking about growth? If so, what are they? What would you say needs to change in your thinking? What counsel do group members give you on this matter?

2. With a group of Christian friends and church members, discuss ways in which you all have been growing lately. In what ways are holy desires and habits being cultivated by God's grace?

3. Which of the strategies for spiritual growth are most needed in your life right now? How will you put them into action?

For Further Reading

Bridges, Jerry. *The Pursuit of Holiness.* Colorado Springs, CO: NavPress, 1978.

Ferguson, Sinclair B. *The Christian Life: A Doctrinal Introduction.* Edinburgh: Banner of Truth, 1981.

Piper, John. *Don't Waste Your Life.* Wheaton, IL: Crossway Books, 2003.

Sproul, R. C. *Knowing Scripture.* Downers Grove, IL: InterVarsity, 1977.

Tripp, Paul David. *Instruments in the Redeemer's Hands: People in Need of Change Helping People in Need of Change.* Phillipsburg, NJ: P&R, 2002.

A HEALTHY CHURCH MEMBER IS
A HUMBLE FOLLOWER

The health of a local church may ride exclusively on the membership's response to the church's leadership. How the congregation receives or rejects its leaders has a direct effect on the possibilities of faithful ministry and church health. Does a congregation appreciate and accept sound preaching? Will its members trust and follow a leader in difficult or unclear situations? Do they rally behind or tear apart the leadership when plans and ideas fail?

In the final analysis, church members are the people who generally make or break a local church. And making or breaking a church has a lot to do with the membership's attitudes and actions toward its leaders.

So no serious attempt to define a healthy church member can neglect reflecting on the interaction between church members and church leaders. And not surprisingly, the inspired Word of God provides ample instruction regarding the *attitudes* and *actions* of church members who wish to contribute to the health of their local congregations by following the leadership of the church.

A Healthy Church Member's **Attitude toward Leadership**

At least three attitudes characterize a healthy church member's when it comes to following a local church's leaders.

1) *Honors the elders.* Several passages of Scripture instruct church members to honor the elders and leaders of the congregation. For example, 1 Timothy 5:17 tells us, "The elders who direct the affairs of the church well are worthy of double honor, especially those whose work is preaching and teaching." What does such double honor include? The apostle Paul brings attention to two things in the following verses. In verse 18, honoring the elders includes caring for their financial and physical needs. A congregation and a member that honor its leadership provide appropriate and sufficient wages for its leaders, particularly those whose full-time labor is ministry to the body.

In verse 19, the apostle indicates that honoring our leaders includes protecting their reputations. We are not to "admit a charge against an elder except on the evidence of two or three witnesses." The apostle understands better than anyone how the ministry is open to charges, criticisms, and complaints from outside and inside the church. A healthy church member will help to shelter the shepherd from unwarranted slings and arrows. Rumors and backbitings die at the ears of a healthy church member who refuses to give consideration to unedifying and uncorroborated tales.

A healthy church member honors the elder's office. He or she esteems it highly, is thankful for it, and respects those who serve the Lord's people as elders. We honor our pastors because on the day of the Lord they shall be our boast (2 Cor. 1:14).

2) *"Shows open-hearted love to the leaders.* The honor and respect a church member gives an elder is not the distant and official honor a soldier gives a commanding officer. Coupled with the honor due a shepherd is an open-hearted love. Repeatedly, Paul called the Corinthian church to open their hearts to him as one who cared for them spiritually:

> We have spoken freely to you, Corinthians, and opened wide our hearts to you. We are not withholding our affection from you, but you are withholding yours from us. As a fair exchange—I speak as to my children—open wide your hearts also. (2 Cor. 6:11–13)

There should be a sweet exchange of affection between pastor and congregation. As they live, grow, and labor together, their hearts are to open increasingly wide to each other. A healthy church member does not "withhold" his affection from the pastor; rather, he gives it freely and liberally.

A healthy church member doesn't want to hear his or her faithful pastor plead like the apostle did with the Corinthians, "Make room in your hearts for us. We have wronged no one, we have corrupted no one, we have taken advantage of no one. I do not say this to condemn you, for I said before that you are in our hearts, to die together and to live together" (2 Cor. 7:2–3).

A healthy member first gives himself to the Lord and then to the minister of the Lord, knowing that this is God's will (2 Cor. 8:5). Such a member sees how the faithful pastor will spend himself for the body in love. And he would be ashamed to hear the pastor ask, "If I love you more, will you love me less?" (2 Cor. 12:15). Unrequited love is fit for Shakespearean tragedy, not the local church. Our rejoicing in and love for our pastors should "refresh their hearts in the Lord" (Philem. 20).

3) *Is teachable.* A healthy church member should also have a teachable spirit. A teachable spirit evidences humility of heart and a desire to grow in Christ. Without it, a people grow stiff-necked and incorrigible.

The leader's job may be boiled down to one task: teaching. If a member or any significant portion of the membership proves unteachable, the shepherd's task becomes a burden, even undoable, since it's opposing him at this most essential point. Writing to Timothy, Paul provides wonderful instruction for pastors that contains good instruction for members as well. Speaking of the role of elder, Paul writes:

> The Lord's servant must not be quarrelsome but kind to everyone, able to teach, patiently enduring evil, correcting his opponents with gentleness. God may perhaps grant them repentance leading to a knowledge of the truth, and they may escape from the snare of the devil, after being captured by him to do his will. (2 Tim. 2:24–26)

Several things from this passage are useful for church members to observe. First, the pastor's instruction is meant to be gentle, kind, and for our good. We should not take sinful advantage of that God-ordained disposition. Rather, we should accept that kind instruction as a rebuke and a call to repentance. A healthy church member doesn't mistake godly kindness for weakness in a pastor, but uses the occasion to examine his or her own heart for areas needing repentance.

Second, we should recognize how easy it is to "oppose" the pastor as he instructs us. As a regular part of our spiritual life, we should ask ourselves, "Am I in any way opposing the teaching of the pastor?" Third, we should pray for knowledge of the truth, clear-mindedness, and protection from the devil's schemes whenever we discover even a kernel of opposition to pastoral instruction. The pastors watch over our souls as a man who must give an account to God; we should then trust and accept their leadership joyfully as a gift from God for our everlasting benefit. Be teachable.

A Healthy Church Member's Actions toward Leadership

In addition to these basic attitudes or dispositions, there are some specific actions a healthy church member will take in order to effectively follow the leadership of a local church.

PATIENTLY PARTICIPATES IN THE SELECTION OF LEADERS

Perhaps the most important decision a congregation makes—assuming a congregational polity—is the selection of its leaders. By choosing leaders, a congregation sets the spiritual tone and direction of the church, sometimes for generations. Perhaps this is why the apostles instructed the early church to look for spiritual qualities and maturity in its leaders (Acts 6:1–6; 1 Timothy 3). Selecting a leader is to be done with patience and prayerful deliberation. "Lay hands on no man hastily" is the apostle's instruction to Timothy (1 Tim. 5:22a). The first deacons were to be "full of the Spirit and wisdom" (Acts 6:3). Discerning these qualities requires prayer, observation, and patience. And if the Lord's church is to be healthy, church members must call and ordain leaders who are spiritually minded and mature in Christ.

Healthy church members do not overlook the importance of this essential task. They may invite the prospective leader and his family to lunch or dinner in order to know him better. They will want to hear more about the man's testimony, about his desire to serve in a leadership capacity, and about his previous ministry in churches. Some churches allow two months between a man's nomination for leadership and the actual vote in order for members to participate in precisely this way.

OBEYS AND SUBMITS TO LEADERS

Here's a good reason to prayerfully and patiently participate in the recognition of church leaders: a healthy church member must obey and submit to her or his leaders. *Obey* and *submit* are not only "bad words" at weddings, they're bad words to many church members. Yet the Bible couldn't be clearer: "Obey your leaders and submit to them" (Heb. 13:17). Our obedience is to make their work a joy, not a burden. And our obedience redounds to our benefit, since it would be of no advantage for us to call men as leaders and then disobey them. A healthy church member orders himself under the leaders of the congregation as a soldier orders himself in the rank and file beneath a military general. We are to joyfully, eagerly, and completely submit to our leaders for our good, their good, and the good of the entire body.

FOLLOWS THE LEADERS' EXAMPLE

One reason the Lord appoints men to leadership in the church is to provide a flesh-and-blood example of faithful, godly living to the congregation. Our leaders are the "motion picture" of following Jesus. They are called to be an example in everything (1 Tim. 4:12; 1 Pet. 5:3). That's why the apostle Paul says, "Brothers, join in imitating me, and keep your eyes on those who walk according to the example you have in us" (Phil. 3:17). A healthy church member patterns his or her life after the godly lifestyle of the elders of the church. We are to follow our leaders' example with the expectation of conformity to Christ.

For many in our day, this very idea of imitation sounds cultish. There are too many personality cults where people parrot all that the celebrity pastor says or does. We're correct to be concerned with such an unbiblical notion of example setting and mentorship. Yet the Bible's picture of following the pastor's example points to genuine godliness "in speech, in conduct, in love, in faith, and in purity" (1 Tim. 4:12) by doing what is good (Titus 2:7). Pastors are called to be such models, and healthy church members wisely follow their pattern of holiness.

PRAYS FOR LEADERS

Given all that church leaders must do and contend with, can you think of a more important thing to do than to pray for them? Even the apostle Paul understood his need for the saints' faithful prayer:

> Continue steadfastly in prayer, being watchful in it with thanksgiving. At the same time, pray also for us, that God may open to us a door for the word, to declare the mystery of Christ, on account of which I am in prison—that I may make it clear, which is how I ought to speak. (Col. 4:2–4; see also Eph. 6:19–20)

We should pray for our leaders' boldness, clarity, and consistency with the gospel message, and for opportunity for them to proclaim Christ. Healthy church members are devoted to prayer on behalf of their leaders. They heed Jesus' exhortation to pray and not give up (Luke 18:1), and they do that on behalf of their shepherds.

In our local church, a faithful band of members meets every Tuesday night for the purpose of praying for leadership. Weekly they solicit prayer requests and updates on previous requests. When they meet, they lift up all kinds of prayers for the personal, public, and ministry lives of the elders. God has produced great fruit in our body through their prayers.

SUPPORTS OUTSIDE MINISTRY AND INTERACTION OF LEADERS

This is perhaps the least obvious of the actions that a healthy church member takes in following leadership. There is a great tendency among church members to be fairly possessive of their pastors—"he's *our* pastor." There are positive aspects to this possessiveness. It shows, for example, an open-hearted attachment to the shepherds.

However, this possessiveness can become selfishness if the congregation refuses to support a pastor's involvement in ministry outside the local congregation. The person most often hurt in such selfishness is the pastor himself, who, without outside stimulation and refreshment from fellow pastors and leaders, tends to dry and shrivel on the vine. A healthy church member contributes to a leader's ongoing health and vigor in the ministry by encouraging participation in outside conferences, speaking opportunities, and fellowship with other church leaders.

The Bible provides ample illustration of one congregation's support of another. A local church's generosity to other churches is commended in 2 Corinthians 9:13. And such generosity, when it takes the form of "loaning" a shepherd in ministry to others, hopefully expands the regions in which the gospel is proclaimed (2 Cor. 10:15–16). A healthy church member wants to see the gospel advanced and wants to contribute to the health of other congregations if possible. Supporting a leader's outside ministry is one way to fulfill this desire.

Conclusion

Leadership in the local church is established by God for the blessing of his people. However, for leadership to be effective, it needs to be encouraged and supported by the members of the church. Many faithful men have shipwrecked on the rocky shoals of incorrigible and resistant members. It ought not to be so among God's people. Rather, healthy members of a local church should strive and encourage others to strive to follow their leaders with wide-open hearts, eager obedience, and joyful submission.

For Further Reflection

1. Consider the instruction to church members in Hebrews 13. In what way has submission to your church leaders brought you advantage or blessing?

2. In what specific ways can you pray for your leaders?

3. How can you encourage other church members to place greater trust in the church's leaders as they follow Christ and teach the word?

For Further Reading

Mahaney, C. J. *Humility: True Greatness*. Wheaton, IL: Crossway, 2005.
Sande, Ken. *The Peacemaker: A Biblical Guide to Resolving Conflict*. Grand Rapids, MI: Baker Books, 2003.

A HEALTHY CHURCH MEMBER IS A PRAYER WARRIOR

When I was a little boy, we used to celebrate our friends' birthdays by giving them spankings, a wallop for each year of their birthday. And then we'd conclude with one extra lick, saying, ". . . and one to grow on." In keeping, the first nine chapters of this book correspond to the nine marks in its companion volumes, *Nine Marks of a Healthy Church* and *What Is a Healthy Church?* while this tenth chapter is "one to grow on."

I can't think of a single Christian I've met who did not believe that prayer is important, and not only important but a vital part of the Christian life. Odd indeed would be the Christian who attempts to live the Christian life without prayer.

But despite its universally accepted status, prayer remains for many Christians a difficult task, a duty without joy and sometimes seemingly without effect. Christians may waver between the poles of neglect and frustration when it comes to prayer.

Why should this be? Why should otherwise healthy Christians and members of churches find prayer such a difficult exercise?

A House of Prayer for All People

Difficulty in prayer becomes all the more disconcerting when we realize that the church is to be a place of prayer. The prophet Isaiah spoke of a time when eunuchs and foreigners would find a welcome home among the people of God. Those from nations outside of Israel would keep the covenant of God, and the Lord promised of these foreigners:

> These I will bring to my holy mountain,
> and make them joyful in my house of prayer;
> their burnt offerings and their sacrifices
> will be accepted on my altar;
> For my house shall be called a house of prayer
> for all peoples. (Isa. 56:7)

The Lord Jesus quoted this promise when "he entered the temple and drove out all who sold and bought in the temple," reasserting that God's house was no place for thieves but for people of prayer (Matt. 21:13; Mark 11:17).

When we survey the activities of the early church recorded for us in Scripture, we discover that one of the central things early church members devoted themselves to was prayer. As they awaited the promise of the Holy Spirit, they assembled in the upper room and "with one accord were devoting themselves to prayer" (Acts 1:14). After Pentecost, when God added to their number those who were being saved, the earliest members of the Christian church "devoted themselves" to four things: "the apostles' teaching and the fellowship, to the breaking of bread and the prayers" (Acts 2:42). The earliest Christians' engagement in prayer was so strong it could only be called "devotion."

As a spiritual discipline, prayer is so important that it's the only devotion given as a reason for interrupting normal marital devotion between husband and wife (1 Cor. 7:5). Can you imagine the revival in spiritual lives that would break out if Christian bedrooms were to find spouses saying, "Not now, honey, let's devote ourselves to prayer" instead of "Not now, honey, I have a headache." From the home to the church, prayer is essential.

What Is Prayer?

But simply pointing out the importance and centrality of prayer in the early church does not make us prayer warriors. Not only that, we can often be confused as to what prayer really is. Wrong ideas abound. For example:

- Unless we pray, God cannot act in the world.
- God has already decided everything; he's sovereign, so why pray?
- God is too busy to listen to my prayers.

At root, most misunderstandings about prayer stem from a misunderstanding about the nature of God and our relationship to him. It's easy to turn prayer into a me-centered stage show where our claims and needs hog the spotlight and God is a stagehand changing the settings at our request. Yet it's also easy to fall off the other side of the wagon by making God a cosmic chess player deterministically moving all the pieces without regard to the actions of his people.

What we need is a gospel-centered understanding of prayer. Theologian Graeme Goldsworthy offers this understanding:

> The gospel is primarily about the work of the Son. How we know the Son will determine how we view our relationship with the Father who speaks to us through his word. How we view that relationship will determine, in turn, how we come to God in prayer and with what confidence. Prayer will never again be a sentimental excursion or an instinctive hitting of the panic button. Nor will it be the presumption of an innate right to demand God's attention. Rather it will be the expression of our entry into God's heavenly sanctuary, which has been procured for us by our Great High Priest.[1]

Believing the gospel changes our status from outsiders to members of the family of God, adopted sons of God through faith in Christ. On this basis—our sonship through faith in Christ—we may speak to God as his redeemed children. "Prayer is our response to God as He speaks to us,"[2] first in the gospel of Christ, and subsequently in his Word.

Prayer is "not pleading a cause before an unwilling God,"[3] and neither is it acting as a surrogate for a god too impotent to effect anything without us. In prayer, as children united with Christ, our advocate and high priest, the heir of all things, we stand before God receiving a full hearing. Because we are before God in Christ, there is no ceiling that blocks our prayers, though we often imagine there is. Rather, "we involve ourselves in the business that God has with the world" by praying "towards the fulfillment of God's revealed purposes for the whole universe" through "the gospel and its God-ordained outcome." Prayer is "thinking God's thoughts after Him"[4]—thoughts that will always be heard and answered.

How and When Shall We Pray?

A lot of books have been written on the subject of prayer. Some prescribe certain methods for prayer. Others examine the prayer lives of people in the Bible or great saints from church history. With so many books on prayer, and knowing how much progress I need to make in my own prayer life, I'm hesitant to offer suggestions for others to consider. But, in God's kindness and mercy, he has told us how and when to pray.

The how and when of prayer boil down to two biblical teachings: pray constantly and pray in the Spirit.

CONSTANTLY

The apostle Paul frequently encouraged the churches to which he wrote to pray constantly. He exhorted the Thessalonians to "pray without ceasing" (1 Thess. 5:17). Paul wrote to the Christians in Rome to "be constant in prayer" (Rom. 12:12). And to the Colossians he wrote, "Continue steadfastly in prayer, being watchful in it with thanksgiving" (Col. 4:2). This was one way those in the Colossian church could set their minds on and "seek the things that are above, where Christ is, seated at the right hand of God" (Col. 3:1–2). As an example, Paul held up Epaphras, who was "always struggling on your behalf in his prayers" (Col. 4:12). In view of the temptations, dangers, and needs of the Christian life, the healthy church member heeds God's command for constancy in prayer.

IN THE SPIRIT

Not only is the healthy church member constant in prayer, she or he also prays in the Spirit. "Praying in the Spirit" is variously understood by different Christian groups, and much confusion exists on this point. But, again, Paul's letter to the Romans is helpful, where he writes: "The Spirit helps us in our weakness. For we do not know what to pray for as we ought, but the Spirit himself intercedes for us with groanings too deep for words. And he who searches hearts knows what is the mind of the Spirit, because the Spirit intercedes for the saints according to the will of God" (Rom. 8:26–27).

The unfortunate result of so much speculation over a passage like Romans 8:26–27 is that the wonderfully encouraging and plain emphasis is overlooked. And there is great teaching here to encourage us in our prayers. Notice that the Spirit "helps us in our weakness." We've already noted that prayer is one area where Christians readily admit their weakness. How kind it is for God the Holy Spirit to help us in precisely this area! Ever find yourself at a loss for knowing what to pray? The Spirit himself intercedes for us. Ever wish you knew exactly what the will of God was so that you could ask for it? It is precisely "according to the will of God" that the Spirit intercedes for us.

All this is a pivotal clue for what it means to pray in the Spirit. Prayer in the Spirit is prayer *controlled* by the Spirit. And prayer controlled by the Spirit is prayer according to the will of God. It is when we pray in accord with God's will, which is revealed in his Word, that we pray in the Spirit. Such prayer is the birthright of everyone born of the Spirit and adopted as sons of God (Rom. 8:14–17). It is by such prayer that we wage our warfare as Christians (Eph. 6:18).

For What and for Whom Shall We Pray?

As we saw in Romans 8:26–27, one of the ways the Spirit of God helps our weakness in prayer is by interceding for us when we do not know what to pray. Nevertheless, the Lord has also told us some things for which we should pray.

PRAY FOR LABORERS AND SHEPHERDS

Matthew's Gospel records for us an instance when Jesus was moved with compassion for the harassed and helpless people of Israel who appeared "like sheep without a shepherd." Jesus immediately instructed his disciples to "pray earnestly to the Lord of the harvest to send out laborers into his harvest" (Matt. 9:36–38). Perhaps only Christians who have been in churches that have suffered through prolonged periods without a pastor know the urgency of this prayer. The Lord's people need shepherds, and healthy church members petition him to send shepherds to their churches and other churches in need of pastors. And not only do they pray that shepherds and laborers would be sent, they also pray that the Lord would help and strengthen those who labor in the Word during times of distress, suffering, and weakness (Phil. 1:19–20); grant boldness to pastors in proclaiming the gospel (Eph. 6:19–20); and grant opportunity for the spread of the ministry and the gospel (Col. 4:3–4).

PRAY FOR ALL THE SAINTS

Praying for other Christians is a tangible expression of love and care (see Eph. 6:18). Christianity is not a solo sport, and prayer is not a trip through the Burger King drive-thru, where we shout into an inanimate receiver, wait a few moments, and then receive the bag of goodies we ordered to "have it our way." The Christian life is a family life, and our prayers are to focus on the entire family, esteeming others more highly than ourselves. One way to do this is to pray regularly through your local church's membership directory, if they publish one. Pray through one page or one letter of the alphabet per day. Another way of praying for all the saints is to pray for other churches in your neighborhood and churches where other family and friends are members. As we meet with the Lord to study his word each day, we can love other Christians by praying the truth of God's Word over their lives each day. We can pray for their sanctification (1 Thess. 4:3); we can pray against temptation and for watchfulness (Matt. 26:41); we can pray that they would be filled with the Spirit (Gal. 5:16–25) and nearly anything else the Bible commends for Christians.

PRAY FOR THOSE IN AUTHORITY

The young pastor Timothy received these words from his mentor, the apostle Paul: "First of all, then, I urge that supplications, prayers, intercessions, and thanksgivings be made for all people, for kings and all who are in high positions, that we may lead a peaceful and quiet life, godly and dignified in every way" (1 Tim. 2:1–3). Given that God ordains all authority in life, from government leaders (Rom. 13:1–2) to parents (Eph. 6:1–3), and given the blessings that God bestows on those who follow the authorities he has ordained, it makes sense that Christians should pray for those in authority. Healthy church members regularly remember in their prayers elected officials, government employees, school teachers, their own employers, parents, and others with authority. It's helpful to keep a list of such persons in your Bible or your prayer journal as an organized reminder to pray for those in authority.

PRAY FOR THOSE WHO ABUSE AND PERSECUTE THEM

This is the Lord's charge: "Bless those who curse you, pray for those who abuse you" (Luke 6:28). It is natural to pray for people we love. Even unbelievers manage such "prayers." But the love of Christ compels us to pray even for those who abuse, slander, and injure us (Matt. 5:46–47). Amazingly, such prayers give evidence that we are sons of God (Matt. 5:45), even as persecution for righteousness is cause for rejoicing because of Christ's promised reward in his kingdom (Matt. 5:10–12). We're not to be like the unmerciful servant, who, though forgiven by his creditor, roughly treated others who owed him (Matt. 18:21–35). We're to fight the fleshly impulse to not love our persecutors and to neglect them in prayer, and we're to choose instead the superior joy and righteousness of the sons of God who pray even for their abusers.

Conclusion

Can there be a more marvelous privilege than that which has been afforded to Christians through Christ: to stand before God our Father and respond in prayer by his Spirit to his Word spoken to us? If we would be expositional-listening, gospel-saturated, biblical theologians, we should pray with the confident knowledge of what God is doing in the world through Christ his Son and pray for the worldwide advancement of his gospel and will.

For Further Reflection

1. Do you have a specific plan for prayer? Review your current plan or write a new plan for prayer that includes:

   a) private and group/public times of prayer;
   b) times and places of prayer;
   c) specific individuals and groups of people to pray for;
   d) gospel and church concerns;
   e) passages of Scripture you find encouraging and helpful in prayer.

For Further Reading

Carson, D. A. *A Call to Spiritual Reformation: Priorities from Paul and His Prayers*. Grand Rapids, MI: Baker Books, 1992.

Goldsworthy, Graeme. *Prayer and the Knowledge of God: What the Whole Bible Teaches*. Downers Grove, IL: InterVarsity, 2003.

Mack, Wayne A. *Reaching the Ear of God: Praying More . . . and More Like Jesus*. Phillipsburg, NJ: P&R, 2004.

Packer, J. I., and Carolyn Nystrom. *Praying: Finding Our Way Through Duty to Delight*. Downers Grove, IL: InterVarsity, 2006.

Ryken, Philip Graham. *When You Pray: Making the Lord's Prayer Your Own*. Phillipsburg, NJ: P&R, 2000.

A FINAL WORD

Writing this book was a blessing and a privilege. I owe much to the teams at 9Marks and Crossway for giving me the opportunity to write it, and especially to Jonathan Leeman and Lydia Brownback for providing help and guidance that cannot be monetized. Thanks are also owed to my fellow laborers in the gospel at First Baptist Church of Grand Cayman; the congregation, staff, and leaders all offer Godward encouragement and model much of what is written here. And without Kristie, a helper suitable for me and a far richer blessing than I deserve, my labors would be less fruitful, joyous, and adventurous. I am deeply grateful to God for his grace and guidance as I penned these chapters. Everything worthwhile in the book results from his work, not mine, and all the dross appears because of my weakness and inability.

As I reflect on my own weaknesses as a Christian, pastor, and church member, I am reminded that you, too, may have weaknesses that affect your reading of this book. Two come to mind in particular.

First, it is entirely possible to read this book and assess yourself while completely losing sight of Jesus Christ and the cross. That is, you may read this book and go away thinking "work, work, work" instead of "grace, grace, grace" or "trust, trust, trust." Each of the chapters may have become for you a roadmap for self-improvement and self-effort, duty and perhaps drudgery.

The counsel of this book is offered not as a prescription to be taken independent of God's grace in the gospel of Jesus Christ. Neither condemnation and judgment nor practical atheism are the hoped-for results of this book. Rather, I pray that you've been able to read *What Is a Healthy Church Member?* with a pleading heart, desiring that the Lord of the church might supernaturally awaken each of his saints to serve in extraordinary ways. I pray that a deep dependence upon the True Vine—apart from whom we can do nothing—grows in each of our hearts as we long more and more to be what Christ is making us to be. However the Lord moves you to put the suggestions of this book into practice, I pray that you would do so with an increasing understanding of and reliance upon the life of Christ now at work in you and the Spirit who seals and empowers the Christian for every good work.

Second, it is entirely possible to read this book with the spirit of individualism. You may finish this book and think, "Let me get to work on me." And to be sure, there is a great deal of growth we all need to make, and by God's grace will make, until Christ returns. But this book is about the church, the whole of Christ's body in a particular place. Much is said about your role and my role in it, but you and I are meant for and belong to all the others who assemble as God's people (Rom. 12:5). So, the best way to put this book into practice is to do so with the partnership, support, and love of other Christians in your local church. Don't be a "Lone Ranger

Christian," exclusively or myopically concerned with you. Lock arms with others who love the Lord and love his church and together grow in the grace and knowledge of our Lord Jesus Christ.

Author Jerry Bridges recalls his understanding of the local church during the early years of his Christian walk. He writes:

> For many years I took an individualistic approach to the Christian life. I was concerned about *my* growth as a Christian, *my* progress in holiness, *my* acquisition of ministry skills. I prayed that God would enable *me* to be more holy in my personal life and more effective in my evangelism. I asked God's blessing on *my* church and the Christian organization *I* worked for. But as I learned more about true fellowship, I began to pray that *we* as the Body of Christ would grow in holiness, that *we* would be more effective witnesses to the saving grace of Christ. It is the entire Body—not just me—that needs to grow.[1]

My hope is that the same switch from "I" to "we" that Jerry Bridges describes would be true for more and more of God's people. I pray that this small contribution would play some part in increasing our love for the body of our Savior and in so doing would lead the church to greater strength, vitality, and health.

APPENDIX:
A TYPICAL COVENANT OF A
HEALTHY CHURCH

Having, as we trust, been brought by Divine Grace to repent and believe in the Lord Jesus Christ and to give up ourselves to Him, and having been baptized upon our profession of faith, in the name of the Father and of the Son and of the Holy Spirit, we do now, relying on His gracious aid, solemnly and joyfully renew our covenant with each other.

We will work and pray for the unity of the Spirit in the bond of peace.

We will walk together in brotherly love, as becomes the members of a Christian Church; exercise an affectionate care and watchfulness over each other and faithfully admonish and entreat one another as occasion may require.

We will not forsake the assembling of ourselves together, nor neglect to pray for ourselves and others.

We will endeavor to bring up such as may at any time be under our care, in the nurture and admonition of the Lord, and by a pure and loving example to seek the salvation of our family and friends.

We will rejoice at each other's happiness, and endeavor

with tenderness and sympathy to bear each other's burdens and sorrows.

We will seek, by Divine aid, to live carefully in the world, denying ungodliness and worldly lusts, and remembering that, as we have been voluntarily buried by baptism and raised again from the symbolic grave, so there is on us a special obligation now to lead a new and holy life.

We will work together for the continuance of a faithful evangelical ministry in this church, as we sustain its worship, ordinances, discipline, and doctrines. We will contribute cheerfully and regularly to the support of the ministry, the expenses of the church, the relief of the poor, and the spread of the Gospel through all nations.

We will, when we move from this place, as soon as possible, unite with some other church where we can carry out the spirit of this covenant and the principles of God's Word.

May the grace of the Lord Jesus Christ, and the love of God, and the fellowship of the Holy Spirit be with us all. Amen.

NOTES

INTRODUCTION

1. If you're a Christian and you're *not* a member of a church, let me invite you to pick up a fabulous book written to help you think through why you should be a member. The book is called *Stop Dating the Church* by Joshua Harris (Sisters, OR: Multnomah, 2004).

MARK 1: A HEALTHY CHRISTIAN IS AN EXPOSITIONAL LISTENER

1. Mark Dever, *Nine Marks of a Healthy Church* (Wheaton, IL: Crossway Books, 2004), 40.
2. Around age 19, Edwards penned the following resolution: "Resolved, When I think of any theorem in divinity to be solved, immediately to do what I can towards solving it, if circumstances do not hinder me." *The Works of Jonathan Edwards, Vol. 1* (Peabody, MA: Hendrickson), lxii.

MARK 2: A HEALTHY CHRISTIAN IS A BIBLICAL THEOLOGIAN

1. J. I. Packer, *Knowing God,* 20th Anniversary Edition (Downers Grove, IL: InterVarsity, 1993), 12.
2. Mark Dever, *Nine Marks of a Healthy Church* (Wheaton, IL: Crossway Books, 2004). See chap. 2.
3. Wayne Grudem, *Systematic Theology* (Grand Rapids, MI: Zondervan, 1994), 26–30.
4. *The New Dictionary of Biblical Theology: Exploring the Unity & Diversity of Scripture*, ed. T. Desmond Alexander, Brian S. Rosner, D. A. Carson, Graeme Goldsworthy (Downers Grove, IL: InterVarsity, 2000).
5. Vaughn Roberts, *God's Big Picture: Tracing the Storyline of the Bible* (Downers Grove, IL: InterVarsity, 2003); Mark Strom, *The Symphony of Scripture: Making Sense of the Bible's Many Themes* (Phillipsburg, NJ: P&R, 2001); Peter Jensen, *At the Heart of the Universe: What Christians Believe* (Downers Grove, IL: InterVarsity, 2003); Graeme Goldsworthy, *According to Plan: The Unfolding Revelation of God in the Bible* (Downers Grove, IL: InterVarsity, 2002); Graeme Goldsworthy, *The Goldsworthy Trilogy: Gospel and Kingdom, Gospel and Wisdom, and The Gospel in Revelation* (Carlisle, UK: Paternoster), 2001.

6. Downers Grove, IL: InterVarsity, 2001– .

7. Edinburgh: Banner of Truth, 1975.

MARK 3: A HEALTHY CHRISTIAN IS GOSPEL SATURATED

1. Mark Dever, *Nine Marks of a Healthy Church* (Wheaton, IL: Crossway Books, 2004), see chap. 3.

2. John Piper, *God Is the Gospel: Meditations on God's Love as the Gift of Himself* (Wheaton, IL: Crossway Books, 2005), 38. Italics in original.

MARK 4: A HEALTHY CHRISTIAN IS GENUINELY CONVERTED

1. See, for example, John 1:12–13; 3:3–8; 6:44; 15:16; Acts 11:18; Eph. 1:13–14; 2:1–9; 1 Pet. 1:23; and 1 John 4:10.

MARK 5: A HEALTHY CHRISTIAN IS A BIBLICAL EVANGELIST

1. Phillip D. Jensen and Tony Payne, "Church/Campus Connections: Model 1," in *Telling the Truth: Evangelizing Postmoderns,* ed. D. A. Carson (Grand Rapids, MI: Zondervan, 2002), 195.

2. Michael P. Andrus, "Turning to God: Conversion beyond Mere Religious Preference," in *Telling the* Truth; see pp. 155–61.

3. Mark Dever, *Nine Marks of a Healthy Church* (Wheaton, IL: Crossway Books, 2004), 124–30.

4. Michael Andrus, "Turning to God," 161–62.

MARK 6: A HEALTHY CHRISTIAN IS A COMMITTED MEMBER

1. Joshua Harris, *Stop Dating the Church* (Sisters, OR: Multnomah, 2004), 13.

2. Mark Dever and Paul Alexander, *The Deliberate Church: Building Your Ministry on the Gospel* (Wheaton, IL: Crossway, 2005), 60–61.

3. Dietrich Bonhoeffer, *Life Together* (New York: Harper and Row, 1954).

MARK 7: A HEALTHY CHRISTIAN SEEKS DISCIPLINE

1. See, for example, 1 Thess. 4:22 and 2 Thess. 3:6, 11.

2. Jay Adams, *Handbook on Church Discipline: A Right and Privilege of Every Church Member* (Grand Rapids, MI: Zondervan, 1974), 16.

3. C. J. Mahaney, *Living the Cross Centered Life: Keeping the Gospel the Main Thing* (Sisters, OR: Multnomah, 2006). See chap. 2.

4. This was the attitude of the ungodly in Romans 1:18, 21 who "suppress the truth" and "did not honor him as God or give thanks to him."

5. See the Appendix for a sample church covenant.

6. See Matthew 18:17 and 1 Cor. 5:4–5.

7. See, for example, Matt. 18:15 and Gal. 6:1.

MARK 8: A HEALTHY CHRISTIAN IS A GROWING DISCIPLE

1. *The Works of Jonathan Edwards*, vol. 1 (Peabody, MA: Hendrickson, 1998), lxii.

2. Mark Dever, *Nine Marks of a Healthy Church* (Wheaton, IL: Crossway Books, 2004), 214.

3. Don Carson, *The Gospel of John: An Introduction and Commentary*, Pillar New Testament Commentary Series (Grand Rapids, MI: Eerdmans, 1991), 517.

4. Ibid.

MARK 10: A HEALTHY CHRISTIAN IS A PRAYER WARRIOR

1. Graeme Goldsworthy, *Prayer and the Knowledge of God: What the Whole Bible Teaches* (Downers Grove, IL: InterVarsity, 2003), 51.

2. Ibid., 16.

3. Ibid., 35.

4. Ibid., 60–61.

A FINAL WORD

1. Jerry Bridges, *The Crisis of Caring: Recovering the Meaning of True Fellowship* (Phillipsburg, NJ: P&R, 1985), 71–72 (italics in the original).

SCRIPTURE INDEX

9Marks

Building Healthy Churches

9Marks exists to equip church leaders with a biblical vision and practical resources for displaying God's glory to the nations through healthy churches.

To that end, we want to see churches characterized by these nine marks of health:

1   Expositional Preaching
2   Biblical Theology
3   A Biblical Understanding of the Gospel
4   A Biblical Understanding of Conversion
5   A Biblical Understanding of Evangelism
6   Biblical Church Membership
7   Biblical Church Discipline
8   Biblical Discipleship
9   Biblical Church Leadership

Find all our Crossway titles
and other resources at
www.9Marks.org